The Way of the Heart

Spiritual Living in a Legalistic World

G. STEVE KINNARD

The Way of the Heart

Spiritual Living in a Legalistic World

The Way of the Heart
Christian Spiritual Formation Series
Volume One

Illumination Publishers International
www.ipibooks.com
ipi

The Way of the Heart
Spiritual Living in a Legalistic World

09 08 07 06 1 2 3 4 5

ISBN 0-9776954-4-1

Cover design and interior layout: Toney C. Mulhollan

Illumination Publishers International
1190 Boylston Street, Newton, Massachusetts 02464
www.ipibooks.com

Contents

Dedication

To friends—tried and true—

Sam and Cynthia Powell
Matthew and Stacy Fridley
C.Mack and Tenetia Mack
Shane and Sara Engel
Phil and Leslie Garrison
Sheridan and Debbie Wright
Phil and Iris Zayas
Donald and Sissy Hanson

Foreword

Prior to September, 1999, I only knew Steve Kinnard as a Bible teacher from New York City. My first memorable encounter with Steve was when he was ministering in Israel. I was on a tour of Israel, and he served as one of our tour guides.

Jerusalem was one of the last stops on our tour, and I had an appointment there. I had been the videographer for a wedding back in the United States for a messianic Jewish friend and his Gentile bride, and had to drop off the videotape to my friend where he worked, in the southern part of Old Jerusalem. The delivery went well, and I was now supposed to catch up with our group in an area near the Wailing Wall. But I had two strikes against me. First, I have no sense of direction. Second, I have serious dyslexia so reading maps isn't much help. As I began moving around the Arab quarter, I decided to ask a man for directions. He walked with me thirty feet or so and pointed me in the right direction. Then things got really crazy, which leads to my encounter with Steve Kinnard, the Advocate For Tourist Rights.

After I started walking, I realized that I was lost again. The hint! The signs said that I was on the Via Dolorosa. From the movies I had watched, it looked just like the road that Jesus was on as he headed towards Calvary. I started videotaping some of this walk, knowing I was still lost. It was like going back two thousand years in time. I felt like a character in a first century movie. Everyone was dressed in ancient garb. Everyone was looking at me. They were wanting something, saying something, selling something. And then, I saw someone pursuing me. It was the man that I had asked for directions. He was now chasing me, yelling things at me I did not understand. "What had I done wrong?" I thought.

The man was angry. I was no longer trying to find my tour group. Instead, I was trying to get away from someone. This involved running past seventeen-year-olds with machine guns (that's Israel for you), sneaking down dark corridors, hiding in shops and then just plain running. Finally I saw some of my friends snacking and enjoying fellowship. With them was Steve Kinnard. There he was—the guy who had illuminated Caesarea Philippi for our group two days before. The tour guide who at Bet Shean taught us ten reasons for trusting the Bible based upon the archaeology of the Holy Land. He was one of the good guys. Steve went straight up to my would-be assailant and talked with him in some tongue that I did not understand. He straightened things out and off the guy went. Evidently, the man made his living from giving directions to tourists, and thought that I had hired him. Had I known this, I would have paid him. But I had probably seen too many movies with guys like him chasing guys like me.

All's well that ends well. During my time in Israel, Steve had illuminated the Holy Lands, the Bible and the modern people of Israel. He had also saved me from an International Incident, which would have headlined as AMERICAN MINISTER HITS MAN WITH CAMERA.

With this book, *The Way of the Heart*, Steve Kinnard has written the kind of book I would be proud to have written. I discovered that we love the same writers, cherish the same verses of Scripture and have learned some of the same lessons from life's experiences. Spiritual formation is undoubtedly the need of the hour in most churches and for most Christians, especially for leaders. While many great books have been written on this topic, too many of them fall short and allow for spiritual passivity. Spiritual passivity is when someone's idea of spirituality allows them to be inactive. Steve directly challenges this notion: "The way of the heart is not the way of passivity. If we go the way of the heart, then we will be more active for God than ever before... It is action that is based on God's grace and not on our own human achievement."

This book will serve as inspiration for many of us to pursue the joys of knowing Christ without enslavement to checklists and do's and don't's. The reader will be invited on an adventure of discovering the meaning of the heart from Scriptures, God, the great commandments, a man after God's heart and more. The journey continues in an exploration of the kind of heart we would seek to have—a heart of desire more profound than all the rules of legalism, high hoops and ritualism could ever inspire.

Often we buck the lessons that God has given us, fight the opportunities for exploring our hearts, resist what would draw us closer to him and think that we have had a victory when we have found a way out of suffering. Without understanding what we have done, we have invented ways to achieve our goals without growing. Our heart has deceived us into embracing a form of pop Christianity which avoids the script that God has written for us. He has often intended for his believers to walk through the flames, wear sheepskins in an arena full of beasts and encounter all sorts of mistreatment, even to become scapegoats so that we could be transformed into the likeness of his Son. Sadly, we western Christians have been so clever that we have played the victim to the hilt by crying foul at suffering, and have never enjoyed the victory that comes through enduring the pain and calmly scorning evil.

The Way of the Heart, as Jesus modeled it, allowed him to suffer expulsion from his hometown, misrepresentation by his contemporaries, then rejection by the crowds, and finally torture and murder. Yet, who is everyone still talking about two thousand years later? Not the whiners, those who kept their beliefs hidden and avoided suffering for their convictions. In order for us to become one of many Jesuses who draw humanity to God the Father, we will need to lock the door to the path of least resistance. Then we shall need much help with our hearts so that we can respond well to expulsion, misrepresentation, rejection or worse.

Just as Steve Kinnard rescued this American Tourist from himself, I believe that he will help many of his readers avoid a mundane and spineless spirituality. For those willing to explore their heart with the light of Christ, I also believe that these pages will help enlighten the seeker. The goal, of course, is Christ formed in us.

–Steve Staten
Chicago, Illinois

Acknowledgements

I acknowledge a debt to the many Christian devotional authors who have influenced me over the years, including:

C.S. Lewis
Frederick Buechner
Philip Yancey
Dallas Willard
Annie Dillard
David Head
Walter Wangerin, Jr.
John Bell
Michael Quoist
Richard Foster
Dietrich Bonhoeffer
Mother Teresa of Calcutta
Francis Schaeffer
Søren Kierkegaard
François Fenelon
Thomas Merton
Henri J. M. Nouwen
Larry Crabb
Brennan Manning
J. R. R. Tolkien

Thanks to:

My family, Leigh, Chelsea and Daniel.

The elders, staff and members of the New York City Church of Christ.

My close friends in the Hudson Valley Region where I am a minister.

My high school English teacher, Mrs. Hickman, who taught me to love reading.

My college professor, Dr. Porter King, who encouraged my writing.

Sifu Karl Romain, Sifu Linda Morrissey, Jiao Lian Russell Rosado, Si Hing Jon Edmond and the staff of Romain's Kung Fu.

Jerri Newman, who helped edit the text.

Douglas Jacoby, who helped edit the text.

Special thanks to:

Toney Mulhollan, for his work editing, formatting and designing the book, and for his help in seeing this book through to publication.

Leigh Kinnard, for reading through the draft and making several helpful suggestions.

Introduction to The Way of the Heart

Prelude to a Journey

Yahweh, my heritage, my cup,
You, and you only, hold my lot secure;
The measuring line marks out delightful places for me,
For me the heritage is superb indeed.
I bless Yahweh, who is my counselor,
And in the night my inmost self instructs me;
I keep Yahweh before me always,
For with him at my right hand nothing can shake me.

So my heart exults, my very soul rejoices,
My body, too, will rest securely,
For you will not abandon my soul to Sheol,
Nor allow the one you love to see the Pit;
You will reveal the path of life to me,
Give me unbounded joy in your presence,
And at your right hand everlasting pleasures.
—Psalm 16:5-11, The Jerusalem Bible

The words of this psalm summarize the goal of this book. They also summarize the goal of our journey with God. This is the treasure for which we search:

- to see God as our heritage and our cup
- to know that God holds our lot secure
- to believe that God has placed us exactly where we belong
- to see God as our counselor who in the night teaches us how to instruct ourselves
- to keep God ever before us
- to be so close to God that our hearts exult and our souls rejoice in him

- to rely upon God to the point that our bodies feel rest in his security
- to know that God shows us the path of life
- to experience unlimited and unequaled joy in God

This is at one and the same time, our journey and the treasure at the end of the journey. This psalm describes a mystical connection with God. It describes something that seems beyond our reach, yet it is within our reach. It describes the way of the heart.

The Journey

> When spirituality is viewed as a journey...the way to spiritual wholeness is seen to lie in an increasingly faithful response to the One whose purpose shapes our path, whose grace redeems our detours, whose power liberates us from crippling bondages of the prior journey and whose transforming presence meets us at each turn in the road. In other words, holistic spirituality is a pilgrimage of deepening responsiveness to God's control of our life and being.[1]
>
> –J. Robert Mulholland, Jr., professor and theologian

> We think there are a thousand things we should be concerned with, but there is actually only one. If we take care of that one thing, all the others will find themselves done. And if we fail to take care of the one thing that is needful, all the others—no matter how successfully we may seem to do them—will fall into ruin. So why are we so torn between matters of the heart and our worldly concerns?[2]
>
> –François Fenelon,
> 17th century French devotional writer

> The spiritual life is a pilgrimage. It is not a pilgrimage, however, to become something we are not, a work of our own doing. It is rather a process of becoming who we already are, that is, who by God's grace we have been made and who through God's grace we will be enabled to become.[3]
>
> –John Westerhoff, professor of theology

Imagine that you are walking alone through some dense woods on a beautiful spring morning that envelopes you with a crisp air that invigorates and energizes. You begin this journey through these woods to find God. You begin by getting lost. You lose yourself in the forest. You feel nothing of the outside world—no cars, no planes, no music, no human voices—only the rustling leaves of the trees that surround you. Since you don't know where God is, you begin to walk. In walking, you hope to find the path to God. You feel the softness of the earth under your feet as you navigate the rocks and the fallen trees along the floor of the forest.

Your journey is soon halted as you come to two roads in the forest. The roads head in different directions. One is a road that has been well traveled and is easy to spot. The undergrowth of the forest has been worn away by the constant flow of travelers on this road. It seems the easy way. It is clearly marked and not difficult to follow. There is no guesswork in following this road. It is the road that is traveled by most. It is marked with a sign that is freshly painted with bright red lettering on a white background that reads, "The Way of Legalism." Is this the path to God?

The other road is hardly discernible from the thick canopy of the forest. It is obvious that few people have traveled down this road. The encroaching forest has almost obliterated this path. There are remains of a sign, fallen over long ago and overgrown by leaves and brush. You recognize the leaves. A voice rings in your ears. It is the voice of an old friend who taught you long ago, "Leaves of three—let them be." This is poison ivy. You grab a stick and carefully push away the leaves and lift the sign back to its place. The lettering on the sign is difficult to read. It has been worn away by seasons of rain and snow. At first it looks like it reads, "he Way o he ear." But that doesn't make any sense. So you take your hand and rub some dirt off the lettering of the sign, revealing an "H" and then a "t." You see now that the last word is not "ear," but "Heart." You keep rubbing until you you reveal the sign's true message, "The Way of the Heart." You choose to travel the path designated "The Way of the Heart." Thus you begin your journey toward God.

What is the way of the heart? The way of the heart is the path to God. It is the narrow path less traveled. It is the path where we allow God to come to us. God finds us on this path; we don't find him. It is not the path of legalism. It is not the way of the law. It is not the path of performance. It is not the path of conforming to other people's opinions about what is best for us spiritually. It is a solitary path traveled by the lone pilgrim who surrenders all that he or she has and journeys down this road to meet the Creator. It is an individual path. Although it is a solitary path, it is also a path along which one finds fellowship with other solitary travelers likeminded on their journey—the journey of discovering God.

In this book we will explore the way of the heart. We will investigate what it means to have a heart for God. We will debunk the claims of the legalistic, performance-based paths to God, and call for a purer, more Biblical journey to find him—the way of the heart. Although many roads invite us, only one will lead us to union with the Eternal Father of our souls. That is the way of the heart.

In this book we will see what Jesus has to say about the way of heart. How does Jesus say we should approach our journey to the Father? We will also look at the heart of the Father, the heart of Jesus, and the heart of the Spirit.

We Are All Spiritual Beings

> "Spiritual" is not just something we *ought* to be. It is something we *are* and cannot escape, regardless of how we may think or feel about it. It is our nature and our destiny.[4]
>
> –Dallas Willard, author and scholar

> If we know much about ourselves, I think we must agree that there is something in us which, in spite of all the efforts of a materialistic psychology, is not accounted for either by the requirements of natural life or those of social life, and which cannot altogether be brought within the boundaries of the intellectual and rational life. Though as it develops, this "something" will penetrate and deeply affect all these levels of our existence, we recognize that it is distinct from them. It is an element, which is perhaps usually dormant; yet is sometimes able to give us strange joys, and sometimes–strange discomforts. It points beyond our visible environment to something else; to a reality, which transcends the time-series, and yet to which we, because of the existence of this quality in us, are somehow akin.[5]
>
> –Evelyn Underhill, spiritual writer

We live in an age of diversity. We can't just have coffee; we're offered every flavor added to our coffee from amaretto to mocha to vanilla. Go into a shoe store and you'll see a selection of shoes for every activity under the sun. Whether it is dressing up for a wedding or climbing mountains in Colorado or playing tennis, golf, soccer, basketball, or any other sport, you can find a shoe to match the activity. We love choices.

We celebrate our diversity as an expression of our individuality. Yet despite our veneer of diversity, every person who has ever walked the face of the earth has at least one thing in common. We are all spiritual beings. Recognition of our spiritual nature elevates us above the animal world toward the world of higher beings. It takes us beyond mere existence toward true living. Dallas Willard, who has written several important books on spiritual formation, notes:

> Yet there is a life higher than natural thought and feeling for which the "living being" in human nature was made. It is the spiritual. Disruption of that higher life wrecks our thinking and valuation, thereby corrupting our entire history and being, down to the most physical of levels. It is this pervasive distortion and disruption of human existence from the top down that the Bible refers to as sin (not sins)—the general posture of fallen humankind. Humans are not only wrong; they are also wrung, twisted out of proper shape and proportion.[6]

Dr. Willard has hit on a very important point—we are spiritual beings. But our recognition of the "spirit" within has been disrupted by sin.

We cannot deny the "spirit" within us. We must see that at our core we are spiritual beings. Too often we feed our fleshly nature more than we feed our spiritual nature. No wonder the flesh wins out. Through God's grace we can conquer the flesh, but we must draw on his power to wage war against the flesh. He will enable us to live godly lives when we focus on growing spiritually. This is the idea of spiritual formation. Spiritual formation helps us focus on maturing the spiritual being that resides in all of us. Through spiritual formation we form Christ in us. Spiritual formation is the way of the heart.

How Do I Become a Spiritual Person?

> The spiritual life, as I understand it, is ordinary, everyday life lived in an ever-deepening and loving relationship to God and therefore to one's true or healthy self, all people, and the whole of creation.[7]
>
> –John Westerhoff, professor of theology

> Without God we cannot. Without us, he will not.
>
> –attributed to Augustine of Hippo, theologian

Just because we are *spiritual* beings does not mean that we are *spiritual* people. There are people who are *human* beings, but in no way, shape or form are they *humane*. Do you want to become a spiritual person? Do you want God's Spirit to control your life? Do you want to be a kingdom[8] person? Dallas Willard writes, "A person is a 'spiritual person' to the degree that his or her life is correctly integrated into and dominated by God's spiritual kingdom."[9] The more we focus on God's Spirit; the more we will become spiritual people. The more we focus on God's kingdom, the more we become kingdom people. Paul admonishes us in Colossians 3:1-2, "Since, then, you have been raised with Christ, set your hearts on things above, where Christ is seated at the right hand of God. Set your minds on things above, not on earthly things. For you died, and your life is now hidden with Christ in God."

To become spirit-filled or kingdom-focused, we must ask God to transform our hearts to become like the heart of Jesus. We must start our journey and head down the pathway toward God. We must walk the way of the heart.

Life is full of choices. For example, consider the topic of physical fitness and diet. A few years ago, I started to exercise to lose some weight. I tried losing weight by following a low carbohydrate diet. I thought this was the right choice. The diet worked. But one morning I went to the refrigerator and saw an orange on one shelf and a stick of butter on another shelf. I realized that on the low-carb diet I could eat the whole stick of butter, but I couldn't eat the orange. I quit the diet that same day and chose another path.

Next, I began cardiovascular exercise. As I began to run, ride my bike, and lift weights, I found that the muscular man hidden underneath a layer of fat and flab started peeking out. This was a better path. Seeing quick results made me want to run farther and ride my bike more consistently. But after a few months, I grew tried of putting one foot in front of the other as I ran or pushing one pedal over the other as I rode. I wanted to find something that would challenge my body and my mind. So I decided to try another path.

I found this new path with my son Daniel. Together, we began to study Kung Fu and Tai Chi at Romain's Kung Fu Academy in Nyack, New York. (My daughter, Chelsea, is also a student there). I found that practicing these arts was a life-changing experience. The more I applied myself to these arts, the more benefits I reaped in a healthier mind and a healthier body. This path challenged me to get in better shape, but it also challenged me to be a better person. I chose a path that would transform my whole person. This is a path that I want to walk for the rest of my life.

Life is full of choices. What choices are you making with your spiritual life? What choices are you making with your heart? Which path are you walking—the path of worldliness or the spiritual path? Which spiritual path are you traveling down—the way of legalism or the way of the heart?

For most of us, a layer of a fleshly, worldly, unspiritual flab has hidden the spiritual person inside. We must train the spiritual person until he starts peeking out. With enough training, the worldly person begins to evaporate. This is taking the path toward God. This is the way of the heart. But we must be sure of two things: first, that we are on the right path and second, that our heart is in the right place as we journey down that path. Just being on the journey doesn't guarantee that we will arrive at the proper destination, but being on the right path with the right heart will.

We must make sure that we are not on the path of legalism, but that we are journeying on the way of the heart. The path of the legalist states that the journey itself will save us. If we pray enough, read enough, visit enough people, study the Bible with enough people, go to enough worship services, then we will be saved. The way of the heart asks why. Why are we on this journey? Why are we reading our Bible? Why are we studying the Bible with this person?

Why are we at this worship service? Why are we visiting this sick person? Both paths believe that it is important to read, pray, visit and evangelize. But on the path of legalism, we do these actions because we are required to do them. When we walk the path of the heart, we do these actions because we desire to do them. That is the difference between the way of legalism and the way of the heart. The way of legalism focuses only on the action. Since we are performing the right action, then we must end up in the right destination. But a spiritual journey is not only about taking the right action; it is also about why you travel the path. This is the way of the heart.

To illustrate this point, think of a coin. It can be any coin: a quarter, dime, nickel or penny. What is the same about every coin? Every coin has two sides. In America, we call one side of the coin "heads" and the other side "tails." Now think of your spiritual life as a two-sided coin. What are the two sides of this coin? One side is the heart. This is our attitude, our focus, and our desire to follow God. The other side is made up of our righteous actions. A coin with only one side is not really a coin. If we only focus on heart and attitude, but never make any decisions about following God that conclude with action, then we don't really serve God. James, the half-brother of Jesus, taught that faith without action is dead, being alone (James 2:17). On the other hand, if we focus on working, working and working for God without having the right heart for him, then our actions will be pointless. We will become like the Pharisees. We need heart and we need action. Two sides of the same coin.

Choosing the Correct Path

> Spiritual growth is the foundation of any kind of "life building."[10]
>
> –Henry Cloud and John Townsend,
> Christian psychologists

Which path will you take? Throughout our lives we are presented with many different roads to travel down. Some of these roads end in the same place. Others take off in different directions and end in different places. Some roads are broad and wide and are built for high-speed travel. Some are twisting, winding roads that must be traveled with great caution. Some are paved and others are unpaved. Some roads are filled with traffic and others are rarely traveled. Some roads are hundreds of years old and some only recently opened. Roads are for traveling. If a road isn't traveled, it soon falls into disrepair. But at the same time, roads that are traveled often must be tended and maintained, or they fall into a state of disrepair.

A few roads I have traveled in my life have left lasting memories. I've traveled on the autobahn in Germany on more that one occasion. This is a major highway that is known for not having any speed limit. On this road you can go as fast as your car will take you. I remember a time when I traveled on this road and passed a police car while traveling above 90 miles per hour. That was a strange sensation.

I also remember driving on the old Jericho road leading from Jerusalem to Jericho. Jericho, in elevation, is the lowest point on the earth. It sits some 1,300 feet below sea level. Jerusalem is a city set on a hill. It sits some 1,500 feet above sea level. The old Jericho road is the quickest drop in elevation of any road in the world. A new highway has been built so that you don't have to take the old road any longer. The new highway is broad and straight and safe and easy. The old road has been used for centuries. It was first traveled by foot, then by cart, then by automobiles. It twists and winds and drops sharply to the right then to the left. It is dangerous and unsafe. But it is a wonderful road. Both roads arrive at the same destination—Jericho or Jerusalem depending on your direction. But the journey is entirely different. The old Jericho road is the scenic route. You can at any moment see a thousand foot drop to your right or to your left. I love this road. It is historic. You have to travel more slowly on this road. You have to be extra careful. You have to play it safe. But this is a road you will never forget.

Life is filled with roads—physical roads and spiritual roads, literal roads and metaphorical roads. Not all roads are the same and they don't all end at the same destination. Some roads will lead to the same place, but the journey on those roads will differ.

Let's go back to the forest we described at the beginning of this chapter. In this forest we were on a quest to find God. This was our spiritual journey. We can follow this journey down one of two paths. Which path do you want to take? One is well traveled, easy to see, easy to walk upon. It is the road of legalism—the path of performance-based religion. Do we choose this path? The other path is difficult to see. It is barely discernible from the rest of the forest. To travel down this path will take intense focus and dedication. This is the way of heart. It is the opposite of legalism. We all have a decision to make—do I follow the way of legalism or the way of the heart?

The Heart—A Symbol of the Inner Life

All of us live an outer life and an inner life. The outer life everyone sees. It is visible to God and everyone else. It is full of action. Not everyone sees the thought behind the action (that's the inner life), but everyone can see the action and the results of the action. The inner life is kept private to the individual. It is between God and us. We share it with a select few. It includes our attitudes. People can't see our thoughts. They can't see our attitudes. God knows our thoughts, our intent and our attitude. God knows our heart. This is the inner life.

The heart is a fitting symbol of our inner life, our inner world. We can't see the heart, but we know that it is there.

The Inner Way versus the Outer Way—Intrinsic Motivation versus Extrinsic Motivation

> Concerning my third petition, by the grace of God and the teaching of holy Church I conceived a very great desire to receive three wounds in my life—that is to say, the wound of true contrition, the wound of natural compassion, and the wound of full-hearted longing for God. Unlike the first two petitions, which I had made with a condition, I asked this third gift very strongly and without any condition.
>
> The first two desires passed from my mind, but the third dwelled with me continuously.[11]
>
> –Juliana of Norwich, spiritual writer and mystic

> Now, the righteousness of the scribes and Pharisees consisted primarily in externals that often involved manipulative control of other people. Instead of this sort of righteousness, Jesus points to an inner life with God that transforms the heart and builds deeply ingrained habits of virtue.[12]
>
> –Richard Foster, spiritual writer

The inner way—intrinsic motivation—is the way of attitude and desire and proper motivation. It is where we ask why we are doing something. The outer way—extrinsic motivation—is the way of performance and legalism. It is the way of the Pharisees and the self-righteous. It is where we try to measure up to an earthly standard imposed on us from the outside. It is where we do works without checking out motivation or without asking why we are doing something.

Dr. David McAnulty, a friend who is a Christian psychologist in Boston, was sharing with me an interesting study that was done on a group of children. One group of children was asked to play with a puzzle without any type of extrinsic motivation being offered to them. They played with the puzzle for the sake of fun and enjoyment of the puzzle. Any motivation that they had to play with the puzzle was intrinsic.[13] Another group of children was asked to play with the same puzzle, but they were offered money for playing with it. This extrinsic motivation was put in place as they began to play. At the end of a certain period of time, this second group was told that they would no longer be paid to play with the puzzle. As soon as the extrinsic motivation was taken away from the children, they stopped playing with the puzzle. They were no longer interested in it.

At the same time that the second group was told that they would no longer get paid to play, the first group was told they could stop playing or could continue to play. It was their choice. The group that was motivated only by the intrinsic motivation of playing with the puzzle for the joy of playing and having fun, continued to play with enthusiasm after they were given the option of ending. They continued to play with the puzzle long after the second group had stopped. This is the difference between intrinsic motivation and extrinsic motivation. Intrinsic motivation is about desire. Intrinsic motivation is about enjoyment. Intrinsic motivation comes from within. Intrinsic motivation is the way of the heart.

Christian Spiritual Formation

> The greatest difficulty in conversion is to win the heart to God, and the greatest difficulty after conversion is to keep the heart with God.... Heart-work is hard work indeed.[14]
>
> –John Flavel, spiritual writer

This is a book of spiritual formation. Theologians use "spiritual formation" to describe the process of maturing in our spiritual lives. Spiritual formation is a life plan for spiritual growth. Do you have such a plan? M. Robert Mulholland defines spiritual formation as "a process of being conformed to the image of Christ for the sake of others."[15] Spiritual formation is a process. We don't just wake up one morning and—*Voila!*—we are mature, spiritual people. We don't have a fairy godmother who waves her magic wand and transforms us into the image of Christ. We must surrender to the process of being conformed to Christ's image. Cloud and Townsend write:

> Sanctification is a process. Paul said he didn't have it yet (Phil. 3:12-13). Peter said the qualities of good character are built over time in increasing measure (2 Peter 1:8). Fruit is the result of walking in the Spirit, as we sow to please the Spirit (Gal. 6: 8-9). Growth takes time, and it takes time to sow to please the Spirit and to grow in the spiritual life. It is not just a switch that someone pulls—off with the old immature me and on with the new totally mature me.[16]

Michael L. Raposa, in his book *Meditation and the Martial Arts,* calls this sanctification or transformation process a "self-administered brain-washing."[17] I like that image. We have to decide that we are going to allow God to change our heart. Raposa writes about this process and says it occurs through:

> A gradual transformation of heart and mind. It takes practice, and that practice involves exercising self-control, but this is tantamount to a self-administered brain-washing only if that implies success in transforming oneself into the kind of person that one wanted to become in the first place.[18]

I would add that it is only successful if it succeeds in transforming us into being the kind of people God wants us to be. This is the process of spiritual formation.

Have you heard of spiritual formation? It is not a new idea. It is an ancient idea. Bruce Demarest, a professor at Denver Theological Seminary, writes:

> From Pentecost on, Christians understood that conversion was just the beginning of a lifelong cooperation with God's work in

> the soul of the believer. The church and the individual played an active part in responding to God's grace, discovering that certain spiritual practices were highly effective in nurturing the inner man. These practices came to be known as the art and ministry of *spiritual formation*, a form of discipleship we are rediscovering today…Spiritual formation is an ancient ministry of the church, concerned with the "forming" or "shaping" of a believer's character and actions into the likeness of Christ.[19]

So spiritual formation is not new, but is it necessary? M. Robert Mulholland, Jr. answers this question in his book, *Shaped By the Word*, by writing:

> Spiritual formation is not an option. Spiritual formation is not a discipline just for "dedicated disciples." It is not a pursuit only for the pious. Spiritual formation is not an activity for the deeply committed alone. It is not a spiritual frill for those with the time and inclination. *Spiritual formation is the primal reality of human existence.* [20]

Wow! That is quite a statement. If spiritual formation is "the primal reality of human existence," then how are we doing at keeping it genuine? How much do we know about spiritual formation? Do we have anyone that can help us in our process of spiritual formation?

Is spiritual formation in the Scriptures? The term itself is not in the Bible. But the idea of being formed into the likeness of Christ is found throughout the New Testament. Richard Foster, who has been writing about spiritual formation for three decades, emphasizes three verses that speak to the direction and goal of spiritual formation:[21]

- Galatians 4:19, "I am in the pain of childbirth until Christ is *formed* in you."[22]
- Romans 8:29, "For those whom God foreknew he predestined to be *conformed* to the image of his Son."
- 2 Corinthians 3:18, "And all of us, with unveiled faces, seeing the glory of the Lord as though reflected in a mirror, are being *transformed* into the same image from one degree of glory to another; for this comes from the Lord, the Spirit." In *The Message*, Eugene Peterson renders this verse, "We are *transfigured* much like the Messiah, our lives gradually becoming brighter and more beautiful as God enters our lives and we become like him."

Another good verse on spiritual formation is Colossians 1: 28-29. Paul writes, "Him we proclaim, admonishing and teaching everyone in all wisdom, in order that we might present everyone mature in Christ. To this purpose I labor with wearisome effort, struggling like an athlete in the Olympic games with all his energy which powerfully energizes me."[23]

Let's break this verse down and take a closer look. The first word in the verse is the word "him." "Him we proclaim." By starting with the word "him," Paul put the emphasis on the message—the message that Jesus is Lord. N. T. Wright, in his excellent commentary on Colossians, notes, "These words serve for Christian preachers and teachers as a constant reminder of their central calling, not (first and foremost) to comment on current affairs or to alleviate human problems, good and necessary as those activities may be, but to announce that Jesus is Lord."[24] Paul has already modeled what needs to be proclaimed in 1:15-23 where he beautifully announces the supremacy of Christ.

The word "proclaim" is *katangellomen* in the original language. The word indicates the official proclamation of the sovereign leader. It is the proclamation of the king. It is the prophetic proclamation. When we pronounce that Jesus is Lord, we need to do so with great confidence. This is the message of the king.

Who is to proclaim this message? Paul uses the word "we." "Him *we* proclaim." Paul believed in team leadership. He mentions the members of his team in Colossians 4:7-14. Paul was the most successful church builder in the New Testament. But he wants everyone to know that he didn't build churches single-handedly. He didn't build churches based on the power of his own charisma. He built churches through teamwork.

Paul then goes on to state how we proclaim Jesus. We do it by admonishing everyone and by teaching everyone. The word "everyone" (literally, "every person") is found three times in this verse. It underscores the obvious conviction of Paul that everyone needs Jesus in his or her life. Admonishment is different from teaching. Teaching focuses on positive instruction. This should always be done before we admonish people. To admonish means, "to correct through instruction and warning."[25] N. T. Wright says that admonishment "most likely includes the idea of the setting of someone's mind into proper order, with the implication that it has been in some way out of joint."[26] When our necks or our backs are out of alignment, we sometimes go to a chiropractor. In the same sense, we sometimes need a spiritual chiropractor. When our spiritual stiff necks are out of alignment with God, admonishment from a loving brother or sister can get us back in spiritual alignment. Finally, Paul states that we admonish and teach "in all wisdom." There is a difference between wisdom and knowledge. Wisdom means that we are going to apply knowledge to our lives in a spiritual way. The goal of admonishing and of teaching is that people stand on their own two feet and make wise, spiritual decisions about their lives.

Then Paul adds this important little Greek word, *hina*. This word is generally translated as "in order to." We proclaim, admonish, and teach in order to "present everyone mature in Christ." This is the goal of our preaching—to present everyone mature in Christ. This is the goal of ministry—to present everyone mature in Christ. Our goal of ministry is very similar to God's goal for humanity as stated by Paul in Colossians 1:22: "to present us to himself—holy, without blemish and free from accusation." God is working to present[27] all disciples to himself as holy, spotless, and without accusation. We are working to present everyone as mature in Christ. Our goal is to help people spiritually. Our goal is to help everyone grow to maturity. Our goal is to help people walk with God consistently. Our goal is to help people stay faithful. Our goal is to help people exhibit the fruit of the Spirit in their lives. Paul spells out even more clearly in chapters three and four that we must help disciples:

- set their hearts and minds on things above (3:1-4)
- put sin to death (3:5-11)
- clothe themselves with Jesus (3:12-14)
- be thankful and grateful (3:15-17)
- be great husbands, wives, parents and children (3:19-21)
- serve like they are serving Christ (3:23-24)
- be devoted to prayer (4:2-6).

If we were to ask Paul to describe to us his experience in spiritual formation, what it was like helping people to become mature in Christ, how easy or difficult it was to help people grow to maturity, Paul's answer would be, "It was hard. It was difficult labor; it was a struggle." Paul wrote that he labored for the purpose of presenting everyone mature in Christ. The word "labor" means to work with wearisome effort or to work to exhaustion.[28] Paul then adds that he *struggled* to present everyone mature in Christ. The root of the word "struggle," *agon,* often refers to an athletic game. Paul knows that to help people reach maturity is extremely hard and difficult labor.

But then Paul adds a little phrase that makes all the difference—*kata ten energeian autou,* "with all his energy." We don't struggle with our own energy. We struggle with the energy of Christ. And this is energy that will never run out. The full phrase reads, "struggling with all his energy which so powerfully energizes me."[29] N. T. Wright notes:

> Paul does not go about his work half-heartedly, hoping vaguely that grace will fill in the gaps which he is too lazy to work at himself. Nor, however, does he imagine that it is "all up to him," so that unless he burns himself out with restless, anxious toil nothing will be achieved. He knows that God's desire is to bring Christians to maturity, *and* that God has called him to have a share in that work. He can therefore work hard without the stressful motivation of either pride or fear. He thus becomes an example of that maturity, both human and Christian, that he seeks under God to produce in others.[30]

To help people reach spiritual maturity is arduous work. But thanks be to God that we do not have to do this work under our own power. Jesus energizes us. He is the source of our power. Jesus helps in the process of spiritual formation. In fact, he energizes the whole process.

The Purpose of This Book—Spiritual Living in a Legalistic World

I began studying the heart about three years ago. At the time, the church where I was a minister was going through many changes. Many members of the church were voicing the need for reform within our ministry. The winds of change were beginning to blow. At first, I had a bad reaction to their requests for change. (I'm confessing my sin here). I thought people were overreacting. Then I began to see how deeply people were hurt. Once I saw the deep hurt in people, I began to reevaluate everything that I had ever learned in the ministry. I began with a study on the heart.

I thought this would be a nice one-year study that would help me work on my inner life. I found that it is a lifetime study, and that

I need continual help to change my heart. I had always been hesitant to study the heart. One of my seminary professors defined the heart as "the seat of the emotions." For most of my life I've tried to distance myself from emotion. I would study scriptures on the mind, but I bypassed scriptures on the heart. But I finally realized that it was time for me to embrace the fact that I, along with everyone else, am an emotional being. I have heart.

So I undertook this study. Along the way I opened a door to a whole new way of viewing the Trinitarian God and his Scripture. I began to see that God is full of heart and his message to humanity is that he wants to give us his heart so that we can live in union with him. I found that heart in the Bible is much bigger than emotion. In fact, to equate heart with emotion is incorrect. It would be like equating faith with belief. Belief is only part of faith. Faith is much bigger, much broader than belief. In the same way, heart is much bigger, much broader than emotion. The study of the heart has changed my life. I believe that it will change your life as well.

The purpose of this book is twofold. First, we will explore and explain the use of the word "heart" throughout the Bible. By understanding how the word heart is used in the Bible (Old Testament, the Gospels, and the rest of the New Testament), we can develop a proper theology of the heart. We can correct any misconceptions that we might have about the heart, and we can strengthen sound convictions about the heart.

Second, we will explore what the way of the heart is and what it is not. We will make practical applications from our study of the heart. The subtitle of the book is *Spiritual Living in a Legalistic World.* We will discover how we can live the way of the heart in the midst of a performance-based world. The way of the heart is not the path of performance and extrinsic motivation. The way of the heart involves attitude and intrinsic motivation. We will learn what the way of the heart is by looking at the heart of the Father, the heart of the Son and the heart of the Holy Spirit. We will look at how Jesus answers a first-century scribe who asked, "What is the greatest of all the commandments?" We will go through some practical lessons on the heart, in which explanations will be offered for what it means to have a heart for the saved, a heart for the lost, a trusting heart, a teachable heart and a grateful heart. We will prepare ourselves for spiritual living in a legalistic world.

A Christian Spiritual Formation Series—The Way of the Heart

> Through it all, God gradually and slowly "captures" the inner faculties: first the heart and the will, then the mind, the imagination, and the passions. The result is the transformation of the entire personality into the likeness of Christ. More and more and more we take on his habits, feelings, hopes, faith, and love.[31]
>
> –Richard Foster, spiritual writer

In most areas of our life, if we want to grow, mature or be educated in something, then we study a particular curriculum on that topic. When I go to my Kung Fu class, there are certain things that I am expected to learn to advance from white sash to black sash. When it comes to spiritual formation, most of us have never had a curriculum to guide our spiritual growth. Some of us might have read books like *The Purpose Driven Life*. These books can be very helpful to get us on the path toward spiritual growth. But that particular book is written for a forty-day period. What happens after the forty days are over? We need a curriculum of Christ-mindedness that carries us beyond forty days or forty weeks or forty months or forty years. We need a curriculum for spiritual growth that can guide us throughout life.

This book is volume one of a four-volume set, a Christian Spiritual Formation Series entitled *The Way of the Heart*. What is the goal of this curriculum? It is to help us become mature in Christ (Colossians 1:28–29, Ephesians 4:11–16). Thus, this curriculum stimulates Christian maturity and growth. The series teaches us to have the same attitude as Christ (Philippians 2:1-5). Thus, this curriculum develops Christ-mindedness. These volumes teach us to have the heart of Jesus. Thus they are called *The Way of the Heart*. When Paul writes to the disciples in Galatia, he says, "My dear children, for whom I am again in the pains of childbirth until Christ is formed in you…" (Galatians 4:14). Paul's goal was to see Christ formed in every disciple. Thus, he believed in a curriculum of spiritual formation.

Volume one in this Christian Spiritual Formation Series is also entitled *The Way of the Heart.* It is subtitled *Spiritual Living in a Legalistic World.* This book explores the topic of the heart both Biblically and theologically. It deals with our motivation and our attitude. It focuses on how we think about God and how we approach God. It is a foundational study for the rest of the series.

Volume two of the Christian Spiritual Formation Series is entitled *Walking the Way of the Heart.* The subtitle, *Practical Lesson on Spiritual Living,* states both the content and purpose of the book—to practically apply some of the principles discussed in volume one to our everyday spiritual lives.

The proposed third volume of the Christian Spiritual Formation Series is entitled *Living the Way of the Heart.* The subtitle is *Spiritual Disciplines for Spiritual Living.* It is about the classic spiritual disciplines and how they can help us walk the way of the heart.

The proposed fourth volume of Christian Spiritual Formation Series is entitled *Maturing in the Way of the Heart.* This book will discuss the Fruit of the Spirit (Galatians 5) and the Christian Graces (2 Peter 1). As we mature in the way of the heart, the Fruit of the Spirit and the Christian Graces should become natural parts of our lives. This book will help us to evaluate whether the Spirit's fruit and God's graces are growing in our hearts.

I hope that you benefit from this first volume in the series. I know that I have grown from writing it. I believe that it is by walking the way of the heart that God forms Christ in our hearts.

A Perfect Heart
(Author Unknown)

Morning sun light of creation
Grassy fields a velvet floor
Silver clouds a shimmering curtain
He's designed a perfect world
I'm amazed at His talents
Stand in awe of one so great
Now my soul begins to sing out
To the source of which it came

Bless the Lord who reigns in beauty
Bless the Lord
Who reigns with wisdom and with power
Bless the Lord
Who reigns my life with so much love
He can make a perfect heart.[32]

Father,

I pray that as I begin this journey down the path marked "the way of the heart" you will show me the exact details I need to focus on so that you can create the heart of Jesus in me. Reveal the way of the heart to me. Give me unbounded joy in your presence. Allow my inmost self to instruct me. Don't let me give up. I know that you will not give up on me. Keep working on me until Christ is formed in me.

Through Jesus
Amen

Endnotes

[1] M. Robert Mulholland, Jr., *Invitation to a Journey: A Road Map for Spiritual Formation* (Downers Grove: Intervarsity Press, 1993), 12.

[2] François Fenelon, translated by Robert J. Edmonson, *Meditations on the Heart of God* (Brewster, Mass.: Paraclete Press, 1997), 39.

[3] John H. Westerhoff, *Spiritual Life: The Foundation for Preaching and Teaching* (Louisville, Kentucky: Westminster John Knox Press, 1994), 36.

[4] Dallas Willard, *The Divine Conspiracy* (San Francisco: Harper San Francisco: 1998), 79.

[5] Evelyn Underhill, *The Essentials of Mysticism and Other Essays* (Oxford: Oneworld Publications, 1999), 221-222.

[6] Dallas Willard, *The Spirit of the Disciplines* (San Francisco: Harper & Row, 1988), 63.

[7] Westerhoff, 1.

[8] The word "kingdom" throughout this book refers to "the rule and reign of God." The kingdom is anything and everything that God rules over. It includes the church, but is not exclusively the church. Dallas Willard writes about the difference between "church" and "kingdom" in his book *Renovation of the Heart* (San Francisco: Harper and Row, 1988), 16. He states, "Churches are not the kingdom of God, but are primary and inevitable expressions, outposts, and instrumentalities of the presence of the kingdom among us. They are 'societies' of Jesus, springing up in Jerusalem, in Judea, in Samaria, and to the furthest points on earth (Acts 1:8), as the reality of Christ is brought to bear on ordinary human life."

[9] Willard, *Spirit of the Disciplines,* 67.

[10] Henry Cloud and John Townsend, *How People Grow* (Grand Rapids: Zondervan, 2001), 78.

[11] Juliana of Norwich, translated with an introduction by M.L. del Mastro, *The Revelations of Divine Love* (New York: Image Books, 1977), 84.

[12] Richard Foster, *Streams of Living Water* (San Francisco: HarperCollins, 1998), 8-9.

[13] This study is found in Edward L. Deci's *Why We Do What We Do: Understanding Self-Motivation* (New York: Penguin Books, 1995).

[14] John Flavel, *Keeping the Heart* (Grand Rapids: Sovereign Grace Publishers, 1971), 5, 12.

[15] Mulholland, *Invitation to a Journey,* 12.

[16] Cloud and Townsend, 110.

[17] Michael L. Raposa, *Meditation and the Martial Arts* (Charlottesville: University of Virginia Press, 2003), 136.

[18] Ibid.

[19] Bruce Demarest, *Satisfy Your Soul* (Colorado Springs, Colorado: NavPress, 1999), 23.

[20] M. Robert Mulholland, Jr., *Shaped By the Word,* Revised Edition (Nashville: Upper Room Books, 2000), 25.

[21] *"The With-God Life: The Dynamics of Scripture for Christian Spiritual Transformation: A RENOVARE International Conference on Spiritual Renewal," Conference Notebook,* (Englewood, Colorado: Renovare, 2005), 39.

[22] The italics in these verses are provided by the author.

[23] The author's own translation.

[24] N. T. Wright, *Colossians and Philemon,* Tyndale New Testament Commentaries (Grand Rapids, Michigan: William B. Eerdmans Publishing Company, 1986), 93.

[25] Fritz Reinecker, translated by Cleon L. Rogers, Jr., *A Linguistic Key to the Greek New Testament* (Grand Rapids: Zondervan Publishing House, 1976), 571.

[26] Wright, 93.

[27] Some scholars believe that this word "to present" carries with it the idea of presenting a sacrifice on the altar of God. In this case, God offers the sacrifice to himself. In Colossians 1:28-29, we, as disciples, offer the sacrifice to God.

[28] Reinecker, 571.

[29] The author's own translation.

[30] Wright, 93.

[31] Richard Foster, *Streams of Living Water*, 51.

[32] Bud John Sons, Inc. Makanume Music. Ooh's and Ah's Music. Dony McGuire. Beba Rambo. 1981.

Part One

A Biblical View of the Heart

Defining "Heart"

The Bible has been called God's love letter to humanity. Since it is God's love letter, it should be filled with references about the heart. And sure enough, in the NIV the word "heart" is found 500 times and the word "hearts" is found 208 times. Do the math. That is 708 references to the word "heart" in the NIV. The word "grace" is found 131 times. The word "soul" is found 129 times. The word "mind" is found 121 times. The word "faith" is found 270 times. In the English Bible, references to the heart are more numerous than references to grace, soul, mind and faith combined. The Bible is a book about the heart.

Chapter One

Defining "Heart" in the Old Testament

Trust in the Lord with all your heart
and lean not on your own understanding;
in all your ways acknowledge him,
and he will make your paths straight.
(Proverbs 3:5-6)

Men look on the outward appearance, but God looks on the heart.
(1 Samuel 16:7)

Above all else, guard your heart,
for it is the wellspring of life.
(Proverbs 4:23)

A Rosy Nose?

"A rose by any other name would smell as sweet."
But what if?
Instead of *rose*,
You asked for a *nose*?
A *rosy nose*?
If you picked a nose
Instead of a rose
Would that smell as sweet?
GSK, 2005

Definitions

What do you think of when you hear, "He played with all his heart!" How about "They don't have much talent on that team, but they have heart." Or what about, "I'd take heart over talent any day of the week." Or, "She gave him her heart, and he stepped all over it."

How we define words is extremely important. Consider this scenario: You are playing in a major league baseball game. You are at the plate looking out at the pitcher waiting for him to deliver his pitch. He throws a fastball on the inside of the plate. You swing the bat as hard as you can swing it. The bat and ball collide, shattering the bat just above the trademark. The baseball heads backwards into the stands. You walk over to your dugout and ask the batboy to bring you another bat. What if he returns carrying a hairy, nocturnal mammal with a three-foot wingspan, sharp teeth, and bad eyesight? You ask, "What's that?" He replies, "A bat!" You respond, "I want a baseball bat, not a hairy, nocturnal animal with sharp teeth and bad eyesight!" The ball boy says, "Well, you have to be more specific next time and say, 'baseball bat.'"

Defining words correctly is very important. Since the Bible was originally written in Hebrew and Greek, with a touch of Aramaic here and there, an English dictionary is not very helpful in defining Biblical terms. It can help clarify the words in the translation of the text, but it doesn't define what was meant in the *original* language. Whenever I hear a preacher say, "I looked this word up in the dictionary and it means…" I cringe. The dictionary does not define biblical terms. You must get behind the English to the original word in the Greek or Hebrew. This is not an easy task. It takes work. But the effort invested in the task will reap great dividends.

How does the Bible define the word "heart?" In the Hebrew Old Testament the word for "heart" is *lev*, and in the Greek New Testament it is *kardia*. The heart is the control center of our spiritual lives. It is also called our "spirit" or our "will" in the Bible. It is our drive, our motivation and our energy. In the movie *Apollo 13*, Tom Hanks' character notices that something has gone terribly wrong with the Apollo spacecraft he is piloting. He radios Mission Control and says, "Houston, we have a problem." He is hoping that the staff of NASA's Mission Control Center in Houston can help them solve the problem with their spacecraft. In our spiritual lives, the heart is our Mission Control. At times, we need to call into our hearts and say, "Heart, we have a problem."

Our hearts are at the center of our spiritual lives. Whether we realize it or not, we live from the heart. Dallas Willard writes:

> We live from the heart. The part of us that drives and organizes our lives is not the physical. This remains true even if we deny it.

> You have a spirit within you and it has been formed. It has taken a specific character. I have a spirit and it has been formed. This is true of everyone.[1]

Our heart drives and organizes our lives. Since it is so central to our well-being, we need to be sure that we take good care of it.

Our heart is our will, our desire, our emotion, our intellect, our drive and our motivation. It is our personality and our personhood. Our heart is what makes us who we are as people. It is what God wants above everything else.

God wants our heart. Before we do anything for him, he wants our heart. Before we sacrifice, he wants our heart. Before our contribution, he wants our heart. Before we go and get a doctorate in theology, he wants our heart. Before we set out on a mission team for Africa, God wants our heart. Before we get down on our knees to pray, God wants our heart. Before we visit the sick in the hospital or the prisoner in jail, God wants our heart. Before we reach out to the prostitute or the drug dealer, God wants our heart. Before we fast, God wants our heart.

What does God want? Our heart.

If the heart is first given to God, then everything else will follow. The heart is who we are deep down. The heart is about being and not about doing. It is about being God's person. It is about being a disciple of Jesus. The heart is about being Spirit-filled. The heart is about being a student of the Word. The heart is about being a spiritual person.

When you have a heart for God, you don't *do* evangelism; you *are* evangelistic. You don't say your prayers; you are a person of prayer. You don't give a weekly contribution; you are a living contribution to God. You don't join a mission team; you are a missionary. Having a heart for God is about being, not just doing.

The Use of "Heart" in the Old Testament

The Bible has much to say about heart. Let's begin by looking at some of the OT scriptures and their use of the word "heart."[2] After that, we will move on to some NT scriptures.

In the OT, heart can be used in the strict, literal sense of the muscle that pumps blood through our bodies. But for the most part, heart is used in the figurative sense. German scholar Fredrich Baumgartel notes, "The heart is the seat of mental or spiritual power and capacities."[3] In my OT classes in seminary, my professors taught me that the heart is the seat of the emotions. It is that and more. It is the innermost part of every woman and man. It is our circuit board or our computer chip. It is what drives us and keeps us going. Therefore, the heart is extremely important in our spiritual lives.

The heart is in the middle of everything

Have you ever known someone who wants to be in the middle of everything? This person wants to be invited to every party, know every little bit of gossip about everyone, and be included in every activity. I've known people like that. Sometimes they are busybodies; sometimes they are extremely caring people who just don't want to be left out. The heart is much like these people. The heart is in the middle of everything. It is the center of our emotions, our intellect, our drive, our will and our intent. The heart is our personhood, our personality. It is who we are as people. Who we are in our hearts is who we really are. If we have a prideful heart, then we are prideful. If we have a lustful heart, then we are full of lust. If we have a self-righteous heart, then we are self-righteous. If we have a pure heart, then we are pure. Whoever we are in our hearts—that is who we are.

Now ask yourself, "What type of heart do I have?" Is it greedy, selfless, prideful, angry, or bitter? Or is it loving, compassionate, prejudice, envious, or pure? We need to take a quality measurement of our hearts. How do we do that?

- Through self-examination.
- By asking others what they see in us.
- By using the word of God as a mirror.

The heart is the seat of the intellect

Wisdom and discernment are stored in the heart. Proverbs 18: 15 reads,

> The heart of the discerning acquires knowledge;
> The ears of the wise seek it out.

When Solomon was chosen to be the third king of Israel, God allowed him one request. Solomon chose a wise and discerning heart. 1 Kings 3:10-12 reads:

> The Lord was pleased that Solomon had asked for this. So God said to him, "Since you have asked for this and not for long life or wealth for yourself, nor have asked for the death of your enemies but for discernment in administering justice, I will do what you have asked. I will give you a wise and discerning heart, so that there will never have been anyone like you nor will there ever be."

These verses demonstrate that the heart is the seat of our intellect. But we can learn a couple of other lessons here as well. First, God can give us a wise and discerning heart. 1 Kings 4:29 reads, "God gave Solomon wisdom and very great insight, and a breadth of understanding as measureless as the sand on the seashore." Second, to receive a wise, discerning heart, we need to ask God for it. James 1:5 notes, "If any of you lacks wisdom, he should ask God, who gives generously to all without finding fault, and it will be given to him." Wisdom is a gift from God. He offers it to anyone. It is there for the taking. We just need to ask God for it. Once it is given, store it within our hearts and become wise and discerning.

The heart is the seat of our will or intent

We plan and purpose and scheme and dream with the heart. It is the seat of our intent. David, the second king of Israel, wanted to build a temple for God in Jerusalem. 1 Kings 8:17-18 records the words of Solomon, his son and successor:

> My father David had it in his heart to build a temple for the Name of the Lord, the God of Israel. But the Lord said to my father David, "Because it was in your heart to build a temple for my Name, you did well to have this in your heart. Nevertheless, you are not the one to build the temple, but your son, who is your own flesh and blood—he is the one who will build the temple for my Name."

The intent of David's heart was to build the temple of God. Though God did not allow him to accomplish this, yet God acknowledged that the intent of David's heart was good. What is the intent of your heart? Is your heart set to do good for God?

The heart is the seat of the emotions

Have you ever had a broken heart? Most of us have. If we are really honest, then it has probably happened more than once. When we have a broken heart, does the literal flesh of our heart rip open? Of course not. But it feels like it is ripping open. That's because the heart is the seat of the emotions. We feel heartsick; we have broken hearts; we have heartaches. When we hurt, we hurt inside.

Different emotions of the heart

Agony of the heart. Jeremiah is known as the weeping prophet. He felt pain inside his heart over the condition of Judah and Jerusalem. As he declares the judgment of God against Jerusalem, Jeremiah lets his audience know that he does not take pleasure in his prophecy. We read in Jeremiah 4:19 how it hurts him deep inside to pronounce judgment on God's people:

> Oh, my anguish, my anguish!
> I writhe in pain.
> Oh, the agony of my heart!
> My heart pounds within me,
> I cannot keep silent.

A tranquil heart. The wise man Solomon notes in Proverbs 14:30:

> A heart at peace gives life to the body,
> But envy rots the bones.

A sad heart. When we are sad, we often show it on our face; but we feel it in our heart. Nehemiah 2:1-2 states:

> In the month of Nisan in the twentieth year of King Artaxexes, when wine was brought for him, I took the wine and gave it to the king. I had not been sad in his presence before; so the king asked me, "Why does your face look so sad when you are not ill? This can be nothing but sadness of heart."

Summary

Since the heart is the seat of our intellect, our intent, and our emotions, it is extremely important that we take care of it. Proverbs 4:23 says, "Watch over your heart with all diligence, for from it flows the spring of life."

Are you diligent about taking care of your heart? Do you see that your spiritual life flows from it? Do you take time to care for it? For those of you who are parents, do you remember what it was like to pick up your firstborn child for the very first time? I remember how I was with our first child and only daughter, Chelsea. I was careful to slip my hand in just behind the back of her head and gingerly pick her up. I handled her like a fragile, priceless work of art. Her first whimper was like the sounding of the starting gun for a 100-meter sprint. I would go into her bedroom at night just to make sure she was still breathing. I was diligent about her care. After a few months, I began to realize that she was not as fragile as I thought at first. I didn't need to handle her so gingerly. But I should always treat my heart like I treated our newborn baby. We cannot relax our diligence, for Satan is standing ready to take a foothold within our hearts.

God is not concerned about our outward appearance. He looks at our hearts.

> But, O Lord almighty, you who judge righteously and test the
> heart and mind,
> let me see your vengeance upon them, for to you I have
> committed my cause.
>
> –Jeremiah 11:20

How do you feel when someone sizes you up because of the way you look—the color of your hair, your waist size, the color your skin, the wrinkles on your face? It's not a good feeling to have someone judge you on outward appearances. But we live in an age where appearances are everything. Even though we say, "You can't judge a book by its cover," we are always judged by our covers. We wear the newest tennis shoe endorsed by the most popular sports celebrity. We have a "swoosh," an "alligator," or a Hilfiger flag on our shirts. We size people up by outward appearances all the time. But God doesn't judge based on outward appearances. He looks at the heart.

When Israel needed a new king to follow Saul, the prophet Samuel went to the family of Jesse to look for the king. Jesse paraded his sons before Samuel. Yet when Samuel looked over all Jesse's sons, he did not see the next king. Samuel inquired of Jesse whether he had any more sons. Jesse was reluctant to introduce Samuel to his youngest son, David. Jesse didn't believe David looked the part of the king. Samuel persisted until he saw David, because he knew that God does not look at the outward appearance of men, but rather at the heart. In 1 Samuel 16:7, God tells Samuel, "Do not consider his appearance or his height, for I have rejected him. The Lord does not look at the things man looks at. Man looks at the outward appearance, but the Lord looks at the heart."

God chose the youngest son of Jesse. He picked the one tending sheep. He chose the one that Jesse, his own father, didn't think was worthy of consideration. But God chose him. God didn't even consider his outward appearance. He looked at his heart.

We major in the externals. God majors in the internals. We notice the hair, the eyes, the physical build, the winning smile, the great sense of fashion, the confident stance, the sharp wit, the laidback manner. We live in an age when the movie star and supermodel rule. God doesn't even notice the externals. He doesn't care if you hair is combed or uncombed, if your shirt is in style or out of style, if your teeth are yellow or white, if your wrinkles have wrinkles or your skin is smooth as a baby's behind. God doesn't care about those things. God looks at the heart. We need to see things the way God sees them.

When God sees your heart, what does he see?

- a pure heart or a lustful heart?
- an open heart or a closed heart?
- a heart that loves correction or a heart that hates instruction?
- a heart that is fully committed to him or a distracted heart?
- a zealous heart or a tired heart?
- a compassionate heart or a cold heart?
- a heart of flesh or a heart of stone?

Right now, God doesn't care what you are wearing. He doesn't care if you are wearing $250 sneakers or are barefoot. God doesn't care if you're wearing a t-shirt or a silk shirt. God doesn't care if your face is perfectly made up or if it is covered with blemishes. God doesn't judge based on outward appearance. God is looking at your heart.

We must seek God with all of our heart

> Perfect devotion requires us not only to do the will of God, but to do it with love. God loves for us to give to him joyfully. In everything he tells us to do, he always asks for our heart. Such a Master is worthy of our joyful service.[4]
>
> –François Fenelon, 17th century French devotional writer

What do you think of when you hear the terms "half-hearted" and "faint of heart?" You probably think of someone who is uncommitted or someone who is not giving his or her best. God doesn't want us to give him only part of our heart. He wants it all.

The last judge of Israel was Samuel. He was the transitional figure from the time of the judges to the rise of the monarchy. He was also a prophet of God. In Samuel's farewell speech to the Hebrew people, he commented on the fact that they had asked God for a king. Samuel knew that this request was going to prove costly for God's people. By asking God for a king, they were rejecting God as king. He challenged them on their thinking and encouraged them to give their whole heart to God. Samuel told the people:

> I have listened to everything you said to me and have set a king over you. Now you have a king as your leader. As for me, I am old and gray, and my sons are here with you. I have been your leader from my youth until this day. Here I stand. Testify against me in the presence of the Lord and his anointed. Whose ox have I taken? Whose donkey have I taken? Whom have I cheated? Whom have I oppressed? From whose hand have I accepted a bribe to make me shut my eyes? If I have done any of these, I will make it right.
>
> "You have not cheated or oppressed," they replied. "You have not taken anything from anyone's hand" (1 Samuel 12: 1-4).
>
> Then Samuel called upon the Lord, and that same day the Lord sent thunder and rain. So all the people stood in awe of the Lord and of Samuel.
>
> The people said to Samuel, "Pray to the Lord your God for your servants so that we will not die, for we have added to all our other sins the evil of asking for a king.'"
>
> "Do not be afraid," Samuel replied. "You have done all this evil yet do not turn away from the Lord, but serve the Lord with all your heart. Do not turn away after useless idols. They can do

> you no good, nor can they rescue you, because they are useless. For the sake of his great name the Lord will not reject his people, because the Lord was pleased to make you his own. As for me, far be it from me that I should sin against the Lord by failing to pray for you. And I will teach you the way that is good and right. But be sure to fear the Lord and serve him faithfully with all your heart; consider what great things he has done for you. Yet if you persist in doing evil, both you and your king will be swept away" (1 Samuel 12:18-25).

To serve God faithfully, means that we must serve him with our whole heart. That means we hold nothing back. We give it all to God. We don't make bargains with God. Israel realized she had tried to bargain with God by asking for a king. How do we do that? By saying:

- God, I'll give you Sundays, but the rest of the week is mine.
- I'll give you my temper and my laziness, but I'm keeping the lustful heart.
- I'll give you my patience, except when it comes to my boss.
- I'll give you my evangelistic zeal, except when I feel selfish.
- I'll give you my whole heart, unless I have a deadline at work.
- I'll give you my best, until I'm distracted by the world.

In Jeremiah 29:13, God says, "When you search for me, you will find me, if you seek me with all your heart." Imagine that you had a disease thought to be terminal, and you had just seen a report from a Swiss researcher saying that he has found the cure for your disease? He has killed the disease agent in laboratory cultures of cells from sick patients, but he has yet to test the cure *in vivo*. What would you do?

Chances are, you would seek out this researcher, learn everything you could about him and volunteer to test the cure. When you are desperate, you do desperate things. Peter Scazzero in his excellent book, *The Emotionally Healthy Church*, writes, "It is said that the most powerful person in the world is one who has nothing to lose."[5] Do you want to find God? Do you want to fix your heart? Get desperate. Seek him out, and invest your whole self or you'll fail to find him. God can only be found when we seek him with all our heart.

In his farewell address to the Hebrew people, the great prophet/judge Samuel gave the same admonishment as Jeremiah when he said, "But be sure to fear the Lord and serve him faithfully with all your heart; consider what great things he has done for you" (1 Samuel 12:24). When we consider all the great things that God has done for us, it makes it easier for us to give him all of our heart.

God instructs our hearts

I will praise the LORD, who counsels me;
even at night my heart instructs me
I have set the LORD always before me.
Because he is at my right hand,
I will not be shaken.

Therefore my heart is glad and my tongue rejoices;
my body also will rest secure...

(Psalm 16:7-9)

God instructs us to guard our hearts against sin. Through the prophet Ezekiel, he admonished the King of Tyre to keep pride out of his heart. Ezekiel records, "Your heart became proud on account of your beauty, and you corrupted your wisdom because of your splendor" (Ezekiel 28:17). Jeremiah delivered the same type of message to Edom, saying, "The terror you inspire and the pride of your heart have deceived you, you who live in the clefts of the rocks, who occupy the heights of the hills" (Jeremiah 49:16).

God instructed the Hebrew people not to forget that he was the Lord their God, because as soon as they forgot, pride would enter their hearts. Deuteronomy 8:10-14 reads:

> Be careful that you do not forget the Lord your God, failing to observe his commands, his laws and his decrees that I am giving you this day. Otherwise, when you eat and are satisfied...then your heart will become proud and you will forget the Lord your God.

Whenever we read the commands of God, we need to be sure that we take God's instruction deep into our hearts. Proverbs 7:2-3 reads, "Keep my commands and you will live; guard my teachings as the apple of your eye. Bind them on your fingers; write them on the tablet of your heart."

Faith in God must dwell in our hearts. Proverbs 3:5-6 notes, "Trust in the Lord with all your heart and lean not on your own understanding; in all your ways acknowledge him, and he will make your paths straight."

Keep watch over your heart

What does it mean to keep watch over something? When I was in tenth grade a friend of mine was in a terrible car accident. He suffered severe head trauma, and he was in a coma. After being in the hospital for several weeks, his parents brought him home to care for him. They had been at the hospital day after day caring for him, and they needed some rest. They asked me if I wouldn't mind staying up with my friend during the night while they got some sleep. I was to listen to his breathing and make sure that he didn't stop breathing. If his condition worsened, then I was to awaken them so that they could be with their son when he died.

I remember shaking with fear at the heavy responsibility of sitting up with my injured friend. I had to keep watch over him during the night. I learned that night what it meant to keep watch over something. To keep watch is to keep constant vigilance. It means that you do not drop your guard. It is to focus on something. We must keep constant vigilance over our hearts.

Why must we keep constant watch over our hearts?

Because our hearts are deceitful

Who deceives you more than anyone else you know? Is it a co-worker or a neighbor? Is a member of your family or a friend in your community? Is it a local politician or real estate agent? Who is the most deceitful person you know? Be careful how you answer, because if you answered with anyone's name other that your own, you are deceived. The person who deceives you more than anyone else is—you! We are all self-deceived. We are self-deceived because we have deceitful hearts.

Jeremiah 17:9-10 reads, "The heart is devious above all else; it is perverse—who can understand it? I the Lord test the heart, to give to all according to their ways, according to the fruit of their doings." This is why we must keep constant vigilance over our hearts. Only by keeping constant guard over our hearts can we keep the deceit out and store the good in the heart.

Because our hearts can be hardened

We must also keep constant guard over our hearts because they can become hard. Exodus 7:13 talks about Pharaoh, "Yet Pharaoh's heart became hard and he would not listen to them, just as the Lord had said." Do you know what happens if you leave wet, soft clay out in the sunshine? The clay becomes hard. The sun evaporates all the moisture from the clay, and it becomes like stone.

It is possible for our hearts to become hard. We cannot leave our hearts exposed to sin. Sin will soak all the goodness out of our hearts and they will become hard like a stone. Whenever we willfully sin, we make our heart a little harder.

A Native American story states that we are all born with a three-cornered stone planted in the middle of our hearts. Every time we do something wrong, that stone turns one turn. The first time it turns it rips at the flesh of our hearts and causes excruciating pain. The next few times it turns; it travels a bit faster and the pain is less. If we keep doing wrong, then the stone will cut a path through the heart so that it turns freely without even being felt.

This is how the heart becomes hard. I don't believe that anyone is born with a hard heart. But over time, the heart is hardened when we make wrong choices and don't reflect on the pain caused by those choices.

> Listen to me, you stubborn-hearted,
> you who are far from righteousness.
> I am bringing my righteousness near,
> it is not far away;
> and my salvation will not be delayed.
> I will grant salvation to Zion,
> my splendor to Israel.
> (Isaiah 46:12–13)

Because our hearts can turn from God

> The LORD says:
> "These people come near to me with their mouth
> and honor me with their lips,
> but their hearts are far from me.
> Their worship of me
> is made up only of rules taught by men."
>
> (Isaiah 29:13)

We must guard our hearts because they can be led away from God. Deuteronomy 17:17 states, "God speaks of the king of Israel and gives this warning: 'He must not take many wives, or his heart will be led astray.'" This is exactly what happened to Solomon. At the beginning of his reign, he asked God for a wise and discerning heart. God granted him that wish. But over time, Solomon's heart turned away from God. We must keep constant vigilance over our hearts to keep them close to God.

But also because our hearts can be converted

After shouting all the warnings and sounding all the alarms about the need to guard the heart, here is a positive thought. As long as we desire to follow Jesus Christ, even if our hearts have become hardened, callous and stubborn, it can become new again. Our hearts can always be brought back to God. In fact, I believe every heart wants to find God.

In one of the most beautiful calls to repentance in the entire Bible, the prophet Joel writes:

> "Even now," declares the Lord,
> "return to me with all your heart,
> with fasting and weeping and mourning."
> Rend your heart and not your garments.
> Return to the Lord your God,
> for he is gracious and compassionate,
> slow to anger and abounding in love,
> and he relents from sending calamity.
> Who knows? He may turn and have pity
> and leave behind a blessing—
> grain offering and drink offerings
> for the Lord your God.
>
> (Joel 2:12-14)

We can have a change of heart. When we do, God is faithful; and he will act on our behalf. It is never too late to turn your heart back to God.

In Psalm 51:17, after David sinned against God and committed adultery and murder, he penned these words of repentance:

> The sacrifices of God are a
> broken spirit;
> a broken and contrite heart,
> God, you will not despise.

God can give us a new heart. In fact, Ezekiel puts the onus on the people to get a new heart. Ezekiel 18:30-32 reads:

> Therefore, O house of Israel, I will judge you, each one according to his ways, declares the Sovereign Lord. Repent! Turn away from all your offenses; then sin will not be your downfall. Rid yourselves of all the offenses you have committed, and get a new heart and a new spirit. Why will you die, O house of Israel? For I take no pleasure in the death of anyone, declares the Sovereign Lord. Repent and live!

I'm old enough to remember the first successful human heart transplant. It was performed by Dr. Christian Baarnard on December 3, 1967 in Capetown, South Africa. Dr. Baarnard transplanted the heart of Denise Darvall, a 25-year-old who had died in a car accident. Her heart was given to Louis Washkansky, a 55-year-old grocer. Washkansky lived only 18 days before he died of pneumonia. At the time this seemed like science fiction. Now it's an ordinary occurrence. Spiritually speaking, God can give us a heart transplant. We can get a new heart and a new spirit. But we have to go to God and ask him for it. Once we ask, he is ready to give us a new heart.

Dear God,

Create in me a new heart. Give me a heart transplant. I know it will be painful, but I need a new heart. And once you have created that new heart in me, strengthen my resolve to guard my heart like a precious jewel. Keep deceit and pride out of my heart. Keep sin out of my heart. Don't let me make the mistake of Pharaoh. Don't let me make the mistake of Solomon. Instead, allow me to store up good in my heart. Let me store up the goodness of your eternal Word in my heart. Let me store up the goodness of godly relationships. Let me store up the goodness of encouraging, positive thoughts. If I feel my heart getting hard, then help me soften it. If I feel my heart being drawn to world, then sound the alarm and draw me back to you. Create in me a new heart, O God, that I may spend my days pleasing you.

In Jesus' name
Amen

Endnotes

1 Willard, *Renovation of the Heart*, 13.

2 In this section I follow the basic outline presented by Fredrich Baumgartel in the *Theological Dictionary of the New Testament*. Friedrich Baumgartel, "*Lev, Levah* in the OT," in the *Theological Dictionary of the New Testament,* Edited by Gerhard Kittel. Translated and Edited by Geoffrey W. Bromiley, Vol. III, (Grand Rapids: Wm. B. Eerdmans Publ. Co., 1965), 606-607.

3 Ibid, 606.

4 Fenelon, 10.

5 Peter Scazzero with Warren Bird, *The Emotionally Healthy Church* (Grand Rapids: Zondervan Publishing House, 2003), 20.

Chapter Two

Defining "Heart" in the Gospels

> Jesus, the very thought of Thee
> With sweetness fills my breast;
> But sweeter far Thy face to see,
> And in Thy presence rest.[1]
>
> —Bernard of Clairvaux, mystic

When we turn to view the use of the word "heart" in the Gospels, we are at a distinct advantage over viewing the word in the Old Testament. The advantage comes with Jesus. By his example, Jesus gives us a living picture of what it means to have a heart for God. Jesus demonstrates how to give your whole heart to God. He teaches about the heart, but more importantly, he lives out what he teaches. Dallas Willard writes:

> And of course it is Jesus above all who *shows* us how to live in the kingdom. Genuine apostolic succession is a matter of being with him, learning to be like him, along with all those faithful ones who have gone before us. Jesus is the ultimate object of imitation.[2]

All of Jesus—his intellect, his will, his drive, his motivation, his emotion, his personality and personhood, his ambition, his spirit, his intent, his soul, his life, his purpose, his mind, everything about him—was totally, absolutely devoted to God. In discussing how people grow, Cloud and Townsend note, "Biblical principles tell us how people grow; Jesus shows us. He gives us a personal and human example we can see and internalize within our hearts. We have a living, breathing picture of how God wants us to live."[3]

An example is a very powerful tool. To model something for someone is far more effective than telling him or her how to do something. It is possible to teach yourself how to play a musical instrument like the guitar or the drums, but having a teacher who can show you how to hold your hands, position your body, and play is a far superior method of learning. The same is true in sports. It is very difficult to tell someone how to throw a football. But it is relatively easy to "show" him how to throw a football. A visual example is instructive and powerful.

You can also see the power of example in the lives of great people. Mahatma Gandhi didn't just tell the people of India how to fight injustice. He showed them by his own life. Mother Teresa of Calcutta didn't just tell the Sisters of Charity how to love the poorest of the poor; she modeled it with her own life. Mother Teresa only owned two items—a mop and a bucket. This symbolized her life. She spent her life caring for the needs of the poorest of the poor. Her example has outlived her life. This is partly because she showed people how to love the poor and created a living legacy.

John Woolman lived in the middle part of the 1700s in New Jersey. He was one of the first abolitionists in America. But Woolman didn't just tell his fellow Americans about the evils of slavery; he showed them by the powerful example of his life. He refused to eat in houses where slaves prepared the meals. He would not help people write their wills if they were going to pass their slaves on to their children. He stood against slavery by his life and by his teaching. There is power in an example.

Jesus modeled what it means to walk the way of the heart. Jesus did far more than just teach about the heart; in his life, we see the heart of God. In John 14:8-9, Philip says to Jesus, "Lord, show us the Father and that is enough for us." Jesus answers Philip, "Don't you know me, Philip, even after I have been among you such a long time? Anyone who has seen me has seen the Father. How can you say, 'Show us the Father?'" To see Jesus is to see the Father. To see the heart of Jesus is to see the heart of the Father.

The Use of "Heart" in the Gospels and in the New Testament

Just as in the OT, in the NT the word "heart" is seldom used to identify the physical organ that pumps blood throughout the body (Luke 21:34, Acts 14:17, James 5:5). The heart is the abode of the spiritual life. It is where the battle for our soul is waged. The word "heart" occurs in 148 passages in the NT. Johannes Behm writes, "The heart is the center of the inner life of man."[4] Thus the word "heart" can express nuances like emotion, intellect, ambition or personality; but within all of these is the idea that the heart is the center of our inner, spiritual life.

The Life of Jesus. Living the Way of the Heart.

There are two ways that we can learn the way of the heart from Jesus. One is by looking at his life and ministry. Jesus lived the way of the heart. As we see his love for God and his love for neighbor, we learn what it is like to live the way of the heart. The second way is by listening to his teachings. Jesus not only lived the way of the heart; he also taught others how to live the way of the heart. One aspect that distinguishes Jesus from other religious teachers who taught the way of the heart is that Jesus' life and teaching are perfectly consistent. Therefore, we should explore both aspects of the way of the heart in the ministry of Jesus. How did he live the way of the heart, and what did he teach about the way of the heart?

Jesus wasn't afraid to ask his disciples to follow him. This meant not only to obey his teachings, but also to follow his example. When given the call to follow Jesus, the disciples didn't just enter into a classroom and listen to Jesus teach for ten to twelve hours a day. They followed him along the way of the heart. They went from village to village, dealing with people in the real world. At times they would sit and listen to a discourse of Jesus. But most of the teaching of Jesus came through life lessons. Jesus would touch a leper, comfort a widow, exorcise a demon, feed the hungry and raise the dead. The disciples were Jesus' apprentices in the real world.

We can't follow Jesus down the dusty roads of Jerusalem or over the grassy pastures of Galilee, but we can follow his example. To follow Jesus means to follow his living example (which lives today through his testimony and is visible in his community) and enter into the real world where people live.

In living the way of the heart, Jesus knew who he was. He was to be before he was to do.

Part of the problem that many of us have in following the way of the heart is that we base our relationship with God on actions, before we establish who we are in the sight of God. In other words, we focus on doing instead of being. We do Christian acts instead of just being Christians. *Being* a Christian must precede *doing* Christian acts. We must know who we are before we do things for God. If we know who we are, then the doing will necessarily follow. We are to be before we are to do.

Jesus knew who he was. His being the Messiah preceded his doing the righteous acts of the Messiah. His being the Son of God preceded his doing the acts of God's Son. In the Gospel of John, Jesus makes several statements where he demonstrates that he understood who he was. These are known as the "I am" statements. In making these statements, Jesus is showing that he first understood who he was, and then his actions followed that understanding. In other words, before Jesus taught the way to God, he modeled the way to God in his own life because he is "the way, the truth and the life" (John 14:6). Before Jesus taught anything about shepherding people, he understood that he was the good shepherd (John 10:11). All the "I am" statements show us that being precedes doing.

The "I am" statements in John's Gospel:

- I am the bread of life—John 6:35, 41, 48, 51.
- I am the light of the world—John 8:12, 9:5.
- I am the gate for the sheep—John 10:7, 9.
- I am the good shepherd—John 10:11, 14.
- I am the resurrection and the life—John 11:25.
- I am the way, the truth and the life—John 14:6.
- I am the true vine—John 15:1, 5.

If we know who we are before God, then what we do for God will be done from the heart. We are disciples of Jesus; therefore, we do righteous acts of discipleship. We are Christians; therefore, we do Christian acts. "Being" comes before "doing." This is the example of Jesus living the way of the heart.

In living the way of the heart, Jesus demonstrates a life that is totally devoted to God.

> Complacency is a deadly foe of all spiritual growth. Acute desire must be present or there will be no manifestation of Christ to His people. He waits to be wanted. Too bad that with many of us He waits so long, so very long, in vain.[5]
>
> —A.W. Tozer, minister and spiritual writer

When the disciples asked Jesus about what seemed to be a secret supply of food to which he alone was privy, his reply was interesting. "My food," said Jesus, "is to do the will of him who sent me and to finish his work" (John 4:34). Jesus had a secret supply of food, but it wasn't physical food. Jesus was talking about spiritual food. His food was to do the will of God. Food sustains us. Food keeps us alive. Food nourishes us. Jesus was sustained and nourished by doing God's will.

Why did Jesus leave heaven and come to the earth? In John 6:38, Jesus said, "For I have come down from heaven not to do my will but to do the will of him who sent me." Jesus came to the earth for the purpose of doing God's will. His heart was devoted to the Father.

Another insight into the total devotion of the heart of Jesus to the Father comes from John 12:27-28. Here Jesus says, "Now my heart is troubled, and what shall I say? 'Father, save me from this hour?' No, it was for this very reason I came to this hour. Father, glorify your name!" As Jesus makes this statement, he has turned his face to the cross and is preparing for his death. His heart is troubled. He struggles with the path that is before him. But he does not choose another path. His accepts his role and accepts the cross. Jesus was devoted to the Father to the point of being willing to die. Jesus devoted his heart fully to the Father.

In living the way of the heart, Jesus demonstrates *agape* love for people.

Jesus came into the world to do the will of the Father. That is seen in his devotion to the Father. But it is also seen in his devotion to people. Jesus loved people. He loved them with an unconditional *agape* love. He had a heart for people. Even when people didn't love him, he still loved them. In Matthew 11:28–30 Jesus extends the invitation, "Come to me, all you who are weary and burdened, and I will give you rest. Take my yoke upon you and learn from me, for I am gentle and humble in heart, and you will find rest for your souls. For my yoke is easy and my burden is light."[6] Jesus was concerned with people. He wanted to lighten their load in life. Even if this meant that Jesus would take on a heavier load, he was willing to do it because of his love for people.

Jesus loved the crowds, and he loved the individual. Luke 7:11-13 tells the touching story of how personal Jesus' love was:

> Soon afterward, Jesus went to a town called Nain, and his disciples and a large crowd went along with him. As he approached the town gate, a dead person was being carried out—the only son of his mother, and she was a widow. And a large crowd from the town was with her. When the Lord saw her, his heart went out to her and he said, "Don't cry."

When Jesus saw the grief of this widow who had lost her only son, his heart went out to her. The Gospels are full of stories like this one. Jesus touched lepers, fed the hungry, healed the sick, talked to strangers, comforted the grieving and had compassion on everyone. Jesus had a heart for people.

In living the way of the heart, Jesus models how to minister to people.

Since Jesus lived a perfect life and left us a perfect example of how to live life, the way he ministered to people is our perfect example of ministry. What are the elements of Jesus' ministry? How can we model our ministry after his? Let's look at the ministry of Jesus and see what we can learn.

> Jesus went throughout Galilee, teaching in their synagogues, preaching the good news of the kingdom, and healing every disease and sickness among the people. News about him spread all over Syria, and people brought to him all who were ill with various diseases, those suffering severe pain, the demon-possessed, those having seizures, and the paralyzed, and he healed them. Large crowds from Galilee, the Decapolis, Jerusalem, Judea and the region across the Jordon followed him (Matthew 4:23-25).

Three participles—teaching, preaching and healing—summarize the Lord's work in Galilee. His was a teaching, preaching and healing ministry. R. T. France writes:

> Jesus' ministry is summarized under three headings: teaching in their synagogues (i.e. biblical exposition, as in

> Luke 4:16ff), preaching the gospel of the kingdom (i.e. public proclamation, as in 4:17), and healing, in which the power of the kingdom of heaven was actually brought into operation (cf. 12:28); John had preached the same message, but in Jesus' ministry what for John was future became present."[7]

Our ministry today should have the same elements as the ministry of Jesus. Are we teaching the precepts of the Bible, preaching the good news of the kingdom and healing the hurt in people's lives? In which of these elements are we the weakest? Let's restore the ministry of Jesus.

> Jesus went about all the cities and villages teaching in their synagogues and proclaiming the good news of the kingdom and healing every disease and every sickness. When he saw the crowds he had compassion on them because they were harassed and helpless as sheep without a shepherd. Then he said to his disciples, "The harvest is plentiful, but the workers are few. Therefore ask the Lord of the harvest to send workers into his harvest" (Matthew 9:35-38).

What motivated Jesus to go from city to city and from village to village, teaching, preaching and healing? Compassion. What should motivate us to go from neighborhood to neighborhood and from house to house, teaching, preaching and healing? Compassion. Jesus saw the people as sheep without a shepherd, harassed and helpless. The word for "harassed" comes from the Greek, *skullein,* and means "flayed or to skinned." It is often translated as "distressed, worried, troubled or harassed."[8]

The word for "helpless" is *riptein* and it means, "to be cast down either from drunkenness or from a mortal wound."[9] This is the condition of sheep without a shepherd. Without guidance, they easily wander from their green pastures and are eaten by predators. Their future is full of danger. The same can be said about people without Jesus. They are helpless; they are without guidance. Their future is full of danger.

Unlike sheep, people can mask their helplessness with fine clothes, money, a successful career, a smile, and look like they have it all together. But Jesus says that on the inside, they are like sheep without a shepherd. Many look successful at first glance. But when you start digging through the veneer, there is bitterness, sadness and hurt. People don't want to look helpless so they find dozens of way to whitewash their helplessness.

We have to be able to see the hurt in people's eyes no matter how hard they try to cover that hurt. We have to understand that without Jesus everyone is helpless, without guidance and without a future. We must be moved by compassion. If we have compassion, then we will embrace the ministry of Jesus and invest our lives in the teaching, preaching and healing ministry of Jesus.

The Teachings of Jesus on Living the Way of the Heart.

How does Jesus teach the way of the heart? First, by his life and by his example. Second, by his teachings. What does Jesus teach about the heart? What does Jesus teach about being a spiritual person? What does Jesus teach about having a relationship with God?

Before we consider these questions, let's look at some misconceptions about Jesus' teaching on the heart. People think different ideas about what it means to have a relationship with God. What are some of these ideas?

- Some think that to have a relationship with God means that we must be perfect. But this is not the case. We will never be perfect. We will always struggle in life. If we had to be perfect to have a relationship with God, then all of us would be disqualified before we even began the race.
- Some think that to have a relationship with God means that we must keep a Bible under our nose all the time, use super-spiritual language that only the initiated can understand, and dress in the most conservative clothes on the market. But walking the way of the heart isn't about clothes or super-spiritual language or even about walking around with a Bible all the time. We need to hide the Word of God in our hearts. We need to dress properly and watch our language, but dress and language need to flow from a heart that is totally devoted to God.
- Some think that to walk the way of the heart means that we can't laugh and can't enjoy life. We need to be serious all the time—stiff and fake. I remember having a conversation once with a highly educated, brilliant man who believed that there

was no place for humor in a sermon. But God gave us a sense of humor to enjoy. Funny things happen in life. Jesus says, "I have come that they might have life and have it to the full" (John 10:10). Abundant life is enjoyable life. When you enjoy something you smile and you laugh.

- Some think that the way of the heart is about hard-line, grit-your-teeth, militaristic disciple-making. It is about checking in every night with a discipling partner who grills you about how you spent your day. He or she questions you about how many people you invited to church, how much you read the Bible and how long you prayed. But this type of discipleship is all about extrinsic motivation. It is killjoy discipleship. It is less about the one-another scriptures and more about being over someone in the Lord. This type of extrinsic motivation is not the way of the heart. The goal of ministry is to mature people to the point where they can stand on their own two feet spiritually. If they have to check in with a discipling partner every day as mandated by the authority in charge, then they are traveling the way of extrinsic motivation. That is the road of legalism. It is not the way of the heart.

So what does Jesus teach about the way of the heart? Let's consider some of his teachings:

In living the way of the heart, attitude is just as important as action.

I imagine that all of us have heard someone defend harboring hatred in his or her heart by saying, "But I'm not hurting anyone by thinking hateful thoughts." But in teaching the way of the heart, Jesus makes it clear that our attitude is just as important as our actions. In Matthew 5:21-22 Jesus says:

> You have heard that it was said of the ancients, 'Do not murder, and whoever murders will be liable to judgment.' But I say to you that everyone who is angry with his brother is liable to judgment. Whoever says to his brother, 'Raka,' is liable to the council. Anyone who says, 'Fool,' is liable to the fiery Gehenna.[10]

This commandment is directed against the action of murder. But Jesus raises the standard by getting behind the action of murder to the attitude of anger and hatred. Jesus directs us not to be angry with our brother or sister. The focus here goes from the act of murder to the heart behind the act. If lies, hatred, prejudice and anger are rooted out, then we can stop murder. Furthermore, we are not to insult our brother or sister. *Raka* and *moros* both generally mean "fool." But the word *raka* is more of a slur on a person's intelligence, while *moros* is more of an attack on his character. Again, if we love our enemies and if we get anger, hatred and prejudice out of our hearts, then we will never degrade people with insults.

In Matthew 5:27-28 Jesus declares, "You have heard that it was said, 'Do not commit adultery.' I say to you—everyone who looks at a woman in a lustful manner has already committed adultery with her in his heart."[11] It was said, "Do not commit adultery," but Jesus says, "Do not lust after another person." In fact, he goes on to say that to lust after someone is to commit adultery in your heart. Here, Jesus heightens the ethic of moral purity in his community. To guard ourselves against adultery, we must not lust. Jesus gets behind the action to the attitude that leads to the action. Since sin begins in our minds, we must control what we put in our minds. We must guard our hearts against sin.

In living the way of the heart, good or evil can be stored in the heart.

> You brood of vipers, how can you who are evil say anything good? For out of the overflow of the heart the mouth speaks. The good man brings good things out of the good stored up in him, and the evil man brings evil things out of the evil stored up in him (Matthew 12:34–35).

The heart is like a cistern; it stores whatever we put into it. We have to be careful what we store there. If we store evil thoughts, then evil thoughts will devour our hearts. Psalm 73:7 reads, "From their callous hearts comes iniquity; the evil conceits of their minds know no limits."

Since evil can be stored in the heart, it is also possible to store good in the heart. Jesus talked about storing up good in the heart. In the parable of the soils, Jesus says, "The seed on the good soil stands for those with a noble and good heart, who hear the word, retain it, and by persevering produce a crop" (Luke 8:15). We can have a good and noble heart. John Eldredge in his book, *Waking the Dead*, states:

> Jesus himself teaches that at least for somebody, the heart can be good and even noble. That somebody is you, if you are his. God kept his promise. God has circumcised our hearts. We have new hearts. Do you know what this means? Your heart is good. Let that sink in for a moment. Your heart is *good.*[12]

Our heart is good if we store up good in the heart. But we have to be careful and not allow our hearts to deceive us. This is the battleground for the heart. This is why we must keep watch over our hearts.

Matthew 9:4 reads, "Knowing their thoughts, Jesus said, 'Why do you entertain evil thoughts in your hearts? Which is easier: to say, 'Your sins are forgiven,' or to say, 'Get up and walk'?" The Pharisees were storing evil in their hearts. What are you storing in your heart? Good or evil?

In Mark 7:18-23 Jesus teaches:

> "Don't you see that nothing that enters a man from the outside can make him 'unclean'? For it doesn't go into his heart but into his stomach, and then out of his body." In saying this, Jesus declared all foods "clean." He went on: "What comes out of a man is what makes him 'unclean.' For from within, out of men's hearts, come evil thoughts, sexual immorality, theft, murder, adultery, greed, malice, deceit, lewdness, envy, slander, arrogance and folly. All these evils come from inside and make a man 'unclean.'"

These are sometimes called "the sins of the heart" because these sins originate in the heart. But we can cleanse our hearts of evil thoughts. One way to cleanse the heart of evil is to focus on storing good in the heart.

In Luke 6:45 Jesus says, "The good man brings good things out of the good stored up in his heart, and the evil man brings evil things out of the evil stored up in his heart. For out of the overflow of his heart his mouth speaks." What is overflowing from your heart? Does your heart overflow with the good stored up in the heart? In order for our hearts to overflow with good, we must focus on storing good in our hearts.

Jesus shows us how radically important it is for us to store up good in our hearts. What are you storing in your heart? You store up whatever you put in the heart. What kinds of books and magazines are you reading? What are you playing on your iPod? What kind of movies are you watching? What do you listen to when you drive your car? Did you know that the average American spends 400 hours a year in the car? What do you do with those hours, besides keeping the car between the lines? If you were to listen to positive, educational audiotapes during that time, that would be the equivalent of two years of college lectures. What a great opportunity to store up good in your heart!

Let me give you another tip on how to store up good in your heart. Write out positive affirmations and Bible verses on 3x5 cards and tape them all over your house, apartment, car or workspace. Positive affirmations are food for the heart. Put a good thought in your mind early in the morning and keep it there all day long. Think thoughts like: "Yes, I can!" or, "If I can, I must; if I must, I will!" or, "I can't" means "I won't."[13] Fuel your day with positive affirmations. In this way, you are storing up good in your heart.

In living the way of the heart, forgive from the heart.

> Forgiveness is God's invention for coming to terms with a world in which, despite their best intentions, people are unfair to each other and hurt each other deeply. He began by forgiving us. And he invites us all to forgive each other.[14]
>
> –Lewis B. Smedes, psychologist and author

In Matthew 18, Jesus tells one of his most penetrating parables—the parable of the unmerciful servant. Peter's question prompts the telling of this parable. Peter asks, "Lord, how many times must I forgive someone who has sinned against me?" This was a very relevant question in the first century. Rabbis often discussed and debated this matter. In the Jewish mind, forgiveness should be offered to the offender a finite number of times. But Jesus taught that forgiveness should be offered an infinite number of times:

> For this reason the kingdom of heaven is like a king who wishes to settle accounts with his slaves. As he went over his accounts, a person was brought to him that owed 10,000 talents, and he could not pay. The Lord ordered him to be sold with his wife and children and all he owned—so payment could be made. The slave fell on his knees saying, 'Have patience with me, and I will repay you everything.' And his Lord had compassion on him and released him and forgave his debt.
>
> That slave went out and found a fellow slave who owed him 100 denarii, and he seized him by the throat, saying, 'Pay me what you owe.' The fellow slave fell down and begged him, 'Have patience with me and I will repay you.' But he refused. He went and threw him in prison until he could pay the debt.
>
> When his fellow slaves saw these events they were disturbed and they went and told the Lord what had happened. Then the Lord summoned him and said, 'Evil slave! I forgave all your debt because you pleaded with me. Should you not have had mercy on your fellow slave as I had mercy on you?' The Lord was enraged and handed him over to be tortured until he could pay his debt. So my Father in heaven will do to you if you do not forgive your brother from the heart.[15]

Although there are several lessons that can be drawn from this parable, Jesus states the point of the parable very succinctly: "So my Father in heaven will do to you, if you do not forgive your brother from the heart." It is a parable about unlimited forgiveness.

The parable is easily summarized. A king was going over outstanding accounts when he discovered that a man owed him 10,000 talents. D.A. Carson puts this debt in perspective:

> We glimpse some idea of the size of the indebtedness when we recall that David donated three thousand talents of gold and seven thousand talents of silver for the construction of the temple. Some recent estimates suggest a dollar value of twelve million; but with inflation and fluctuating precious metal prices, this could be over a billion dollars in today's currency.[16]

This was an overwhelming debt. The point is that the man could work for the king all his life and still not repay the debt. Does that sound familiar? Hopefully it doesn't sound like your personal debt. But it does sound like the debt that we owe God.

The king ordered that the man, his wife and children should all be sold into slavery to recover the debt. This was in keeping with Old Testament teaching (Exodus 22:3). The man threw himself on the mercy of the king. His life and the life of his family would not come close to paying the debt, as the top price for a slave in that day was about one talent. So the king released him, forgiving his debt. Notice that he did not release him with the expectation of working until the debt was paid. He forgave the debt—nothing was owed.

This same man finds a fellow slave who owes him 100 denarii. A denarius was a day's pay. So he was owed one hundred days' wages. Instead of forgiving his fellow slave, the man had him thrown in prison. The other slaves were greatly distressed at the man's lack of forgiveness, and they reported the incident to the king. The king arrested the man, had him tortured and thrown in jail. Since he was unwilling to forgive others, he would not be forgiven.

The message is clear—we must show forgiveness to others. Lewis B. Smedes writes:

> But why is Jesus so tough on us?
>
> He is tough because the incongruity of sinners refusing to forgive sinners boggles God's mind. He cannot cope with it; there is no honest way to put up with it.
>
> So he says: if you want forgiving from God and you cannot forgive someone who needs a little forgiving from you, forget about the forgiveness you want.[17]

If we are disciples, we should realize how much God has forgiven us. We are the man who owed 10,000 talents to the king. This is a debt that is beyond our ability to repay. So Jesus paid it for us. How ungrateful we are when we turn around and fail to forgive others. As God has forgiven us, we must forgive everyone around us.

In living the way of the heart, we must love God with all our heart.

> Our devotion to God must never stop. We must put it into practice everywhere—in things we do not like, in things that disturb us, in things that go against our point of view, our inclinations, our plans. True devotion holds us ready to give God everything—our well-being, our fortune, our time, our freedom, our life, and our reputation. To be willing to give of

> ourselves in this way, and to accept the consequences, is to be truly devout.[18]
>
> –François Fenelon, 17th century French devotional writer

> Jesus replied, 'Love the Lord you God with all your heart and with all your soul and with all your mind.' This is the first and greatest commandment (Matthew 22:37-38, also see Mark 12:30, Luke 10:27).

We are going to study this verse extensively in chapter ten. If you wish, you can go there now and study it. I mention this verse here because it is central to Jesus' teaching on the heart. In fact, it might be the most important verse on the topic. If we are following Jesus in the way of the heart, then we will love God with all our heart, soul, mind and strength. In other words, we will give God everything that we have. One way to check and see if we love God with all our heart is to ask, "Where is my treasure?" We place our treasure in areas where we are deeply devoted. In the Sermon on the Mount, Jesus says:

> Do not treasure up for yourselves treasures on earth where moth and rust destroy and where thieves break in and steal. Treasure up for yourselves treasures in heaven, where neither moth nor rust destroy, and where thieves do not break in and steal. For where your treasure is, there your heart will be[19] (Matthew 6: 19-21).

Jesus makes it clear that where our treasure is, our heart will be also. So find your treasure, and you will find your heart. Or, find where your heart is, and you will find your treasure: they go hand in glove. What is your passion? What do you dream about? Where does most of your time and energy go? If you asked your closest friends, what would they say makes you really happy? If you asked your acquaintances at school or work, what would they say fires you up? Answer these questions, and you have found your treasure.

Another way to gauge the strength of our devotion is by looking at our purity. But I'm not speaking of purity as just controlling our sexual lust, although that is part of the picture; I'm speaking of purity as single-minded focus. In Matthew 5:8, Jesus says, "Fortunate are the single-minded, for they will see God."[20] Most translations translate this as, "Blessed are the pure in heart, for they will see God." We usually think of purity as an absence of lust, especially sexual lust; but the term means so much more. Purity in the Bible means single-mindedness. Dietrich Bonhoeffer, in his excellent book, *The Cost of Discipleship,* answers the question "Who is pure in heart?":

> Only those who have surrendered their hearts completely to Jesus that he may reign in them alone. Only those whose hearts are undefiled by their own evil, and by their own virtues too. Only they will see God, who in this life have looked solely unto Jesus Christ, the Son of God. For then their hearts are free from all defiling fantasies and are not distracted by conflicting desires and intentions.[21]

Purity is the ability to keep our focus on God and not let our eyes wander over to the distractions of the world. When God is our focus, then everything else in life is in the proper focus. Søren Kierkegaard, the Danish philosopher, wrote a book entitled *Purity of Heart Is To Will One Thing.* Kierkegaard emphasizes that purity must incorporate a single-minded focus on God. What are your greatest distractions in life? How do these distractions keep you from focusing on God? How can you rid yourself of these distractions so that you can be keenly focused on God?

To walk the way of the heart means that we are whole-heartedly devoted to God. Where is your treasure? Where is your focus? Find your treasure and your focus, and you will find your heart. To be whole-heartedly devoted to God we must place all our treasure in him and all of our focus on him.

In living the way of the heart, we must banish doubt from our hearts.

Be faithful. Be positive. Don't give into negative thinking. Such slogans can be found in every self-help volume in the bookstore. But just because modern self-help gurus have appropriated them, does not invalidate these teachings expounded by Jesus throughout his ministry. In fact, where do you think Norman Vincent Peale got the idea of the power of positive thinking? It is not a new idea. It is found throughout the ministry of Jesus.

Matthew records an account of a time when the disciples of Jesus were unable to drive a demon out of a little boy. The disciples question Jesus as to why they were unable to perform this miracle.

In Matthew 17:20 Jesus replies, "Because you have so little faith. I tell you the truth, if you have faith as small as a mustard seed, you can say to this mountain, 'Move from here to there' and it will move. Nothing will be impossible for you."[22]

Jesus rebukes his disciples for their lack of faith. He calls them unfaithful and perverse. He adds, "How long must I be with you? How long must I put up with you?" Jesus could tolerate many things from his disciples: ingratitude, lack of compassion, pride, and selfish ambition; but there was one thing that Jesus could not tolerate—lack of faith.

Why was this? Our lack of faith keeps God from working powerfully in our lives. God often works in spite of our pride. He often works in spite of our lack of compassion. But he will not work through us if we lack faith. Faith is the crucial ingredient to allow God to work through us.

Follow me, do not turn back.
Follow me, leave the dead to bury the dead.
Follow me, and I will make you fisher-men.
Follow me, take up my cross.

Where does He lead? Where is his path?
It leads to the leper–unloved, untouched, alienated.
It leads to the sinner–guilt-ridden, crushed, lost.
It leads to the poor–hungry, naked, sick, hopeless.
It leads to the Christian brother–weak, struggling, faithless.

No wonder I shudder, I hesitate, I draw back.
Who can follow in that path? Who can bear that cross?

"Lo, I am with you always!"
Dear Jesus, help my unbelief.

–GSK, written c.1978

Dear Father,

Please form in me the heart of Jesus. I thank you for his example of what it means to be wholeheartedly devoted to you. Help me to focus on what I need to be, and not just on what I need to do. Help me to embrace the idea that being precedes doing. Help me to walk in Jesus' steps. Help me to internalize his teachings on the heart. Help me to store good in my heart. Help me to forgive from the heart. Help me to have a pure heart that is free of doubt and insecurity, lust and selfish ambition, hatred and pride. Create in me a pure heart, O God. Create in me the heart of Jesus.

In Him
Amen

Endnotes

1 Attributed to Bernard of Clairvaux, translated by Edward Caswell. Kenneth W. Osbeck, *101 Hymn Stories: the Inspiring True Stories Behind 101 Favorite Hymns.* (Grand Rapids: Kergel Publications, 1982), 139.

2 Willard, *The Divine Conspiracy*, 351.

3 Cloud and Townsend, 81.

4 Johannes Behm, "*Kardia* in the New Testament." *Theological Dictionary of the New Testament*, Edited by Gerhard Kittel. Translated and edited by Geoffrey W. Bromiley, Vol. III, (Grand Rapids: William B. Eerdmans Publ. Co., 1956), 611. In this section I follow the basic outline presented by Johannes Behm on pages 611-614.

5 A. W. Tozer, *The Pursuit of God* (Harrisburg, Pennsylvania: Christian Publications, 1948), 17.

6 Many verses describe the compassion of Jesus toward those who are harassed and helpless. See Matthew 9:36, 14:14, 15:32, 20:34; Mark 1:41, 6:34, 8:2; Luke 15:20; James 5:11.

7 R. T. France, *Matthew: Tyndale New Testament Commentaries* (Grand Rapids: William B. Eerdmans Publishing Company, 1985), 174.

8 Reinecker, 28.

9 Ibid.

10 The author's own translation.

11 The author's own translation.

[12] John Eldredge, *Waking the Dead: The Glory of a Heart Fully Alive* (Nashville: Thomas Nelson Publishers, 2003), 69.

[13] I learned these positive affirmations in my martial arts training at Romain's Kung Fu. These positive ideas help me to stay focused during strenuous training sessions. They also have helped me in my daily living.

[14] Lewis B. Smedes, *Forgive and Forget: Healing the Hurts We Don't Deserve* (San Francisco: Harper San Francisco, 1984), xv –xvi.

[15] The author's own translation.

[16] D.A. Carson, *The Expositor's Bible Commentary with The New International Version, Matthew*. 2 vols. (Grand Rapids: Zondervan, 1995), 406.

[17] Smedes, 150.

[18] Fenelon, *Meditations on the Heart of God,* 11.

[19] The author's own translation.

[20] The author's own translation.

[21] Dietrich Bonhoeffer, *The Cost of Discipleship* (New York: Macmillan, 1963), 96.

[22] The author's own translation.

Chapter Three

Defining "Heart" in the Remainder of the New Testament

What does Paul have to say about the heart? What say the Apostle Peter and the Apostle John? What does James, Jesus' half-brother, have to say about the heart? By looking at the life and teaching of Jesus, we have seen the living example of what it means to have a heart for God. But the other New Testament writers have much to say in how to take the teaching of the Gospels and apply them to a life of discipleship. The members of the early church submitted their hearts to the Lordship of Jesus. Our understanding of "heart" would be incomplete without considering what the early disciples had to say about it.

In turning now to the writings of Peter, John, James, Paul and other early church leaders, we are going to come across some of the same concepts that were expressed in the Old Testament and in the ministry of Jesus. Instead of skipping over these repetitious ideas, I have chosen to include them. Why? Because repetition is good for us. Because we learn through repetition. In Kung Fu class we repeat the same forms over and over. We repeat them until they become a conditioned response. My teacher, Sifu Karl Romain, often says, "Repetition is the mother of skill. The more you do it, the better you get. The better you get, the more confidence you have." To learn a skill you have to keep repeating it. Repetition is the mother of skill. In the Bible, ideas are repeated so that as we consider them over and over, they might become part of our heart.

Other New Testament Scriptures that Teach the Way of the Heart

The heart is the house of our emotions and feelings, our desires and passions.

- Joy is centered in the heart, and it is a gift of God. In Acts 14:17, Paul and Barnabas say of God:

> Yet he (God) has not left himself without testimony: he has shown kindness by giving you rain from heaven and crops in their seasons; he provides you with plenty of food and fills your hearts with joy.

- Sorrow and pain reside in the heart. Paul gives us insight into his own inner turmoil over the lostness of the world, writing:

> I speak the truth in Christ—I am not lying, my conscience confirms it in the Holy Spirit—I have great sorrow and unceasing anguish in my heart. For I could wish that I myself were cursed and cut off from Christ for the sake of my brothers, those of my own race, the people of Israel (Romans 9:1-4).

When we experience sorrow or anguish over the lostness of the world, we feel it in our hearts.

In 2 Corinthians 2:4, Paul expresses his concern over the condition of the church in Corinth by writing, "For I wrote you out of great distress and anguish of heart and with many tears, not to grieve you but to let you know the depth of my love for you." Paul felt things deeply. He cared about people. He wanted the best for people. When he experienced pain over the condition of people's spiritual well-being, he felt it in his heart.

- We can fill our hearts with love for others. In Philippians 1:7, Paul shares his love for the disciples in Philippi: "It is right for me to feel this way about all of you, since I have you in my heart; for whether I am in chains or defending and confirming the gospel, all of you share in God's grace with me."
- Sinful desires can take root in the heart. In Romans 1:24, Paul writes, "Therefore God gave them over in the sinful desires of their hearts to sexual impurity for the degrading of their bodies with one another." James 3:14 reads, "But if you harbor bitter envy and selfish ambition in your hearts, do not boast about it or deny the truth." We have to guard our hearts because evil can take root there. One of the best ways to keep darkness out of our hearts is to fill it with light.

The heart is the center of the intellect and understanding. It is the source of thought and reflection.

> For the word of God is living and active. Sharper than any double-edged sword, it penetrates even to dividing soul and spirit, joints and marrow, it judges the thoughts and attitudes of the heart (Hebrews 4:12).

The word of God works as a surgeon's blade to cut into our heart to see what thoughts and attitudes live there. It can help us discern between the good attitudes that we need to keep in the heart and the bad attitudes that we need to expel from the heart.

The heart is the center of our will, our drive and our resolve.

> It is the "will" aspect of personal/spiritual reality that is its innermost core. In biblical language the will is usually referred to as "heart." This it is that organizes all the dimensions of personal reality to form a life or a person. The will, or heart, is the executive center of the self.[1]
>
> –Dallas Willard, spiritual writer and theologian

The heart is our driving force. The heart is our control center. The heart is the center of our volition. When we have a tough decision to make in our lives, we struggle in our hearts over that decision. I'm sure that we have all experienced this. When we are faced with a life-changing decision, we feel anxiety deep inside at our core. We feel it in our heart.

Consider the following verses:

- 2 Corinthians 9:7, "Each man should give what he has decided in his heart to give, not reluctantly or under compulsion, for God loves a cheerful giver."
- Acts 11:23, "When he (Barnabas) arrived and saw the evidence of the grace of God, he was glad and encouraged them all to remain true to the Lord with all their hearts."
- 1 Corinthians 4:5, "Therefore judge nothing before the appointed time; wait till the Lord comes. He will bring to light what is hidden in darkness and will expose the motives of men's hearts. At that time each will receive his praise from God."

The heart is the center of our spiritual lives. The battle for the soul occurs in the heart.

Theo Sorg, a German scholar, writes, "The most significant instances of *kardia* in the New Testament occur in those passages which speak of man's standing before God. The heart is that in man which is addressed by God. It is the seat of doubt and hardness as well as of faith and obedience."[2]

Consider the following passages:

- Romans 8:27, "And he who searches our hearts knows the mind of the Spirit, because the Spirit intercedes for the saints in accordance with God's will."
- Revelation 2:23, "I will strike her children dead. Then all the churches will know that I am he who searches hearts and minds, and I will repay each of you according to your deeds."
- 2 Corinthians 3:3, "You show that you are a letter from Christ, the result of our ministry, written not with ink but with the Spirit of the living God, not on tables of stone but on tablets of human hearts."

Protecting the heart.

Since the heart is the center of our spiritual lives, it is very important that we protect it. In Kung Fu, whenever we practice any form that simulates a blade art (kali sticks, knives, sword), we hold the weapon with one hand and use the other to cover the heart. The latter is called the sacrifice hand because you must be willing to sacrifice that hand to protect the heart from a direct hit. Just as we protect our physical heart against harm, we must also protect our spiritual heart from harm. We should be willing to do anything to protect our hearts.

In Colossians 3 and 4, Paul describes 6 ways that we can help protect the heart. Let us consider them in turn.

Protect the heart by keeping it focused on things above and not on earthly things.

> Since, then, you have been raised with Christ, set your hearts on things above, where Christ is seated at the right hand of God. Set your minds on things above, not on earthly things. For you died, and your life is now hidden with Christ in God. When Christ, who is your life, appears, then you also will appear with him in glory (Colossians 3:1-4).

Paul is saying that we have already risen in Christ. We have put to death the old life, and we now live a new life in Christ. But to stay on target and to protect our hearts, we should always keep our minds focused on things above. To set our hearts and to set our minds means to focus. What is your focus in life? Where do you direct your attention? Where is your heart? Where is your mind? My Kung Fu instructor, Sifu Romain, says, "What you focus on in life, you get!" This is true. Therefore, we must decide every day to focus on God. This daily decision protects our hearts.

I remember a time not long ago when I sat down to have a quiet time with the Lord and something interesting happened. I read a spiritual book, but it just didn't feed me. It was a book that had been highly recommended by many different people. I read a chapter of this book, but I couldn't connect with it. I found myself wanting more. So I picked up my New Testament and turned to Galatians and started reading it out loud. I was preaching the book of Galatians to myself. Reading the Bible out loud is a great way to get more from your Bible study. I finished Galatians and went onto Colossians. I preached to myself for so long that I forgot to eat breakfast. I preached so long that my throat became sore and my voice grew hoarse. But that morning I set my mind on things above. Setting my mind that morning carried me through the rest of the day.

Some time after that event, the same thing happened. I was reading a nice spiritual book thinking that it would be enough to feed my spirit. It was a very positive book with many helpful illustrations. I enjoyed reading it. But I could tell that it was not feeding my spirit. I needed a deeper focus. So I picked up my Greek New Testament and started reading the Gospel of Mark. I read about the ministry of Jesus. By focusing on Jesus, I was able to feed my spirit and to set my mind for the day. I read all the time. I read all kinds of books. But when I really want to feed my spirit and to redirect my focus, I always come back to one source—I come back to Jesus.

Protect the heart by taking off the dirty clothes of sin.

> Put to death, therefore, whatever belongs to your earthly nature: sexual immorality, impurity, lust, evil desires and greed, which is idolatry. Because of these, the wrath of God is coming. You used to walk in these ways, in the life you once lived. But now you must rid yourselves of all such things as these: anger, rage, malice, slander, and filthy language from your lips. Do not lie to each other, since you have taken off your old self with its practices and have put on the new self, which is being renewed in knowledge in the image of its Creator. Here there is no Greek or Jew, circumcised or uncircumcised, barbarian, Scythian, slave or free, but Christ is all, and is in all (Colossians 3:5-11).

To protect our hearts, we need to take off and discard our dirty, sweaty, stinky clothes. After you exercise, you don't want to wear your stinky sweat clothes for the rest of the day. This will cause all kinds of problems. (Problems not just for yourself, but also for anyone around you). I recently read an article about cycling that surprised me. The author stated all the basic problems that cyclists experience during the cycling season. He also stated the reasons for those problems and their cures. The number one problem that can disable a cyclist during the season is not muscle strain or wrecks or aching backs. The number one problem is chafing. The cause of this problem is not poor alignment of the seat or handlebars. The cause is not too much time in the saddle. I was shocked at the number one cause of the problem. The number one cause of the number one reason that keeps cyclists off their bikes is poor hygiene. After rides, cyclists tend to sit around in their dirty, sweaty clothes too long. After a ride, the cyclist needs to immediately change clothes and take a shower. Take off the dirty clothes.

Look again at Colossians and you will see two commands in these verses: "put to death" (verse 5) and "rid yourself" (verse 8). We are to put to death sexual sins—sexual immorality, impurity, lust, evil desires, greed. We are to rid ourselves of sins—anger, rage, malice, slander and filthy language. N. T. Wright notes:

> To put something to death you must cut off its lines of supply: it is futile and self-deceiving to bemoan one's inability to resist the last stage of a temptation when earlier stages have gone by unnoticed, or even eagerly welcomed.... Rather, every Christian

> has the responsibility, before God, to investigate the lifelines of whatever sins are defeating him personally and to cut them off without pity.[3]

Temptation comes to us in stages. We must say no to every stage of the temptation to keep sin away. This is how we put sin to death.

Sin can enslave the heart. Evil thoughts come from the heart. Lust and evil desires can reside in the heart. When we allow those sinful desires to take residence in our hearts, then they are going to make their way into our lives. Paul writes about the Gentiles in Romans 1:24-25 saying:

> "Therefore God gave them over in the desires of their hearts to sexual impurity for the degrading of their bodies with one another. They exchanged the truth of God for a lie, and worshipped and served the created things rather than the Creator—who is forever praised. Amen.

By rejecting God altogether, our foolish hearts will become even darker. We can choose to fill our hearts with light or to allow them to be smothered by darkness. Paul writes, "For although they knew God, they neither glorified him as God nor gave thanks to him, but their thinking became futile and their foolish hearts were darkened" (Romans 1:21). Paul repeats this same idea in Ephesians 4:18: "They are darkened in their understanding and separated from the life of God because of the ignorance that is in them due to the hardening of their hearts."

The heart can become hard to the point that it is disobedient and unruly. It can become unfaithful. The Hebrew writer urges: "See to it, brothers, that none of you has a sinful, unbelieving heart that turns away from the living God. But encourage one another daily, as long as it is called today, so that none of you may be hardened by sin's deceitfulness" (Hebrews 3:12-13). Encouragement from other disciples can keep sin out of our hearts. Or we can miss the fellowship and risk sin taking over our hearts. But we have to be careful because sin can harden our hearts. We can even reach the point where our hearts are unrepentant. Paul writes in Romans 2:5, "But because of your stubbornness and your unrepentant heart, you are storing up wrath against yourself for the day of God's wrath, when his righteous judgment will be revealed."

Protect the heart by clothing it with new clothes

> Therefore, as God's chosen people, holy and dearly loved, clothe yourselves with compassion, kindness, humility, gentleness and patience. Bear with each other and forgive whatever grievances you may have against one another. Forgive as the Lord forgave you. And over all these virtues put on love, which binds them all together in perfect unity. Let the peace of Christ rule in your hearts, since as members of one body you were called to peace. And be thankful. Let the word of Christ dwell in you richly as you teach and admonish one another with all wisdom and as you sing psalms, hymns and spiritual songs with gratitude in your hearts to God. And whatever you do, whether in word or deed, do it all in the name of the Lord Jesus, giving thanks to God the Father through him (Colossians 3:12-17).

Once we take off the old, sweaty, soiled clothes of sin, then we must protect our hearts by putting on new clothes. These new clothes are the clothes of compassion, kindness, humility, gentleness and patience. All of these are bound together by love. Again we see the need to put positive ideas into our hearts. It is not enough just to sweep the heart clean of anything that contaminates it. We must disinfect the heart. We must purify it. We must feed our hearts a continual healthy diet of positive thoughts and positive ideas.

Protect the heart by living a new life in the home.

> Wives, submit to your husbands, as is fitting in the Lord.
>
> Husbands, love your wives and do not be harsh with them.
>
> Children, obey your parents in everything, for this pleases the Lord.
>
> Fathers, do not embitter your children, or they will become discouraged
>
> (Colossians 3:18-21).

Our real selves come out when we are at home. When we are at home, we drop our guard. Our major character flaws come out. Our habitual sins engulf us. Therefore, we have to fight to be different at home. We need a heart transplant in our home life. We need a major attitude adjustment. We need Christ formed in us. Even as I write this, I'm preaching to myself. I had an argument just a short while ago with my wife, and I'm having a difficult time shaking off the aftereffects of that fight. I want to avoid her. I want to spend the day at the music store or the bookstore. But what I need to do is to love my wife. I need a heart transplant. So I'm going to stop typing, and I'm going to pray for a new heart. Then I'm going to give my wife a hug and tell her I love her....

That went great. She was very surprised. It took less than five minutes of my time, but I set the stage for the rest of the day to be a productive day. As you read this, is there anything separating you from your spouse? If so, pray for God to change your heart. Then put down this book and go give your spouse a big hug, and let them know how much you love them. Then come back and read on.

Most scholars believe that Paul was never married and did not have any children, but he offers excellent advice on how to live spiritual lives at home. He identifies areas that create chronic problems: domineering wives, unloving and harsh husbands, disobedient children and discouraging parents. The tone of the home is set by the relationship of the husband and wife. The idea presented is one of mutual love and respect. Husbands need to love their wives. They need to let their wives know that they are appreciated. If wives are loved, then it is much easier for them to respect the husband. Wives should not be control freaks. They shouldn't try to commandeer leadership of the home. Smart couples lead together, each person fully utilizing his or her individual gifts to make the partnership more effective. This allows each person to mature in Christ in a loving, accepting environment.

Paul has a word for the children. He treats them like they are a part of the church. He appeals to their heart. He asks them to please the Lord by being obedient to their parents. He doesn't just bark out the command—*obey!* But he lets them know what makes God happy. God is pleased when children obey their parents. Notice the appeal to the heart.

Next, Paul has a word for the parents. He uses the word "father," but the word can refer to both parents—the father or the mother. Paul tells the parents not to embitter or provoke their children because this leads to discouragement. N. T. Wright has some excellent words on this point:

> Paul refers to the constant nagging or belittling of a child...the refusal to allow children to be people in their own right instead

> of carbon copies of their parents or their parents' fantasies. Children treated like this became 'discouraged' or 'dispirited': hearing continually, both verbally and non-verbally, that they are of little value, they come to believe it, and either sink down in obedient self-hatred or over-react with boastful but anxious self-assertion. The parents' duty is, in effect, to live out the gospel to the child: that is, to assure their children that they are loved and accepted and valued for who they are, not for who they ought to be, should have been, or might (if only they would try a little harder) become. Obedience must never be made the condition of parental 'love'; a 'love' so conditioned would not deserve the name.[4]

I have read dozens of books on parenting, but I don't think I've ever read a single paragraph that summarizes the role of the parent better than that.

Paul teaches us that we can protect the heart by living a new life at home. So much of who we are is based on our life at home. If we can make home a safe haven, then our homes will be a place where we can energize our hearts.

Protect the heart by serving the Lord.

> Slaves, obey your earthly masters in everything; and do it, not only when their eye is on you and to win their favor, but with sincerity of heart and reverence for the Lord. Whatever you do, work at it with all your heart, as working for the Lord, not for men, since you know that you will receive an inheritance from the Lord as a reward. It is the Lord you are serving. Anyone who does wrong will be repaid for his wrong, and there is no favoritism.
>
> Masters, provide for your slaves with what is right and fair, because you know that you also have a Master in heaven (Colossians 3:22-4:1).

Is there anything that can embitter the heart more than feeling like you are someone's slave? If you have ever worked in a job or been in a relationship where someone has taken advantage of you, then you know that feeling. But Paul is not talking about a feeling. He is talking about reality. Paul is speaking not of a job or a relationship, but he is speaking directly to people who were slaves. Paul did not advocate social revolution. He preached a revolution of the heart. Paul tells the slaves to obey their masters. But he teaches obedience with the right attitude. Paul was teaching slaves how to walk the way of heart. They were to work for their masters, picturing their master as being Jesus himself. They were to work for an inheritance from the Lord. Slaves had no rights. They did not have an inheritance. But if they served their masters as if they were serving the Lord, then Jesus would give them an inheritance as a reward. The key is the heart; it is the attitude. You have to envision that you are serving the Lord.

Paul also has a word for the masters. He gives them an attitude check. He tells them to remember that they are also slaves. They have a Master in heaven. Since they are slaves to the heavenly Master, they should make it a point to treat their own slaves fairly. Fair treatment of other people begins with a heart change.

Protect the heart with prayer.

> Devote yourselves to prayer, being watchful and thankful. And pray for us, too, that God may open a door for our message, so that we may proclaim the mystery of Christ, for which I am in chains. Pray that I may proclaim it clearly, as I should. Be wise in the way you act toward outsiders; make the most of every opportunity. Let your conversation be always full of grace, seasoned with salt, so that you may know how to answer everyone (Colossians 4:2-6).

Prayer can protect our hearts. But the prayer that Paul mentions here is outward focused. Paul asks them to prayer for his missionary efforts. He wants to get out of prison so that he can proclaim the mystery of Christ to more people. He challenges them to remember how they should act to people who aren't Christians, making the most of every opportunity with people outside the church.

God can change our hearts.

> One of those listening was a woman named Lydia, a dealer in purple cloth from the city of Thyatira, who was a worshiper of God. The Lord opened her heart to respond to Paul's message (Acts 16:14).

God can soften our hearts. God can renew our hearts. The word of God can pierce our hearts. 2 Peter 1:19 describes this process, "And we have the word of the prophets made more certain, and you will do well to pay attention to it, as to a light shining in a dark place, until the day dawns and the morning star rises in your hearts." Put the Word of God in your heart. Let it sit there and marinate for a while. In time, the morning star with rise in your heart. God will renew your heart.

When we open our hearts to God, his Spirit can dwell in our hearts. Paul in 2 Corinthians 1:21-22 writes. "Now it is God who makes both us and you stand firm in Christ. He anointed us, set his seal of ownership on us, and put his Spirit in our hearts as a deposit, guaranteeing what is to come."

Galatians 4:6 reads, "Because you are sons, God sent the Spirit of his Son into our hearts, the Spirit who calls out, 'Abba, Father'" (Also see 2 Corinthians 1:22). God not only puts his Spirit in our hearts, but when the Spirit comes into our hearts, God's love also takes residence in our hearts. Paul writes, "And hope does not disappoint us, because God has poured out his love into our hearts by the Holy Spirit, whom he has given us" (Romans 5:5). When God's Spirit lives in us, Christ takes residence there as well. Ephesians 3:16-17 reads, "I pray that out of his glorious riches he may strengthen you with power through his Spirit in your inner being so that Christ may dwell in your hearts through faith." Instead of sin ruling in our hearts, the peace of God can rule there. Colossians 3:15 reads, "Let the peace of Christ rule in your hearts, since as members of one body you were called to peace. And be thankful."

I cannot recount the number of times that I have taken a tired, weary, worn-out, unspiritual and un-spirit-filled heart to God for renewal. He has never failed me. He always gives me a renewed heart.

The Heart and Passivity

> A divinely transformed heart, by its very nature, will produce right action. It simply cannot do otherwise.[5]
>
> –Richard Foster, spiritual writer

This is a good place to talk about the heart and passivity. In the past, I was afraid that if I spent too much time talking about the "heart", it would lead to passivity—a lack of action. I feared that people might take scriptures like Psalms 46:10, "Be still and know that I am God," too literally, and they might sit around waiting for God to tap them on the head before they did anything. How are we to think about the heart and passivity?

We must guard against passivity.

> Passivity was for the Israelites, and it is for us one of the greatest dangers and difficulties of our spiritual existence. The land promised to them was one of incredible goodness—'flowing with milk and honey,' as it is repeatedly described. But it still had to be conquered by careful, persistent, and intelligent human action, over a long period of time.[6]
>
> –Dallas Willard, spiritual writer and theologian

By walking the way of the heart, we become more active, not less active. But our activity is God-centered, Jesus-focused, and Spirit-driven activity. It is not activity just to be active. It is not activity without thought or emotion. It is about doing things for the right reason and with the right motivation.

For years, when I was down and out spiritually and when I didn't want to share my faith or read my Bible, I was advised to go do it anyway and my heart would follow. Well I went and did it anyway. I shared when I didn't feel like sharing. I prayed when I didn't feel like praying. I sacrificed when I didn't feel like sacrificing. I did things just to do things and you know what, I wish that I could say that my heart did follow, but for the most part, it did not follow. It didn't follow at all. My heart didn't get right, because I wasn't working on my heart. I was following a legalistic form of righteousness that was a deathtrap. Extrinsic motivation forced me on my feet, but my heart was still asleep in bed. I just got more and more hypocritical. My religion became a heartless religion.

If your heart isn't right, then stop and work on your heart. 1 Corinthians 13:1-3 reads:

> If I speak in the tongues of men and of angels, but have not love, I am only a resounding gong or a clanging cymbal. If I have the gift of prophecy and can fathom all mysteries and all knowledge, and if I have a faith that can move mountains, but have not love,

> I am nothing. If I give all I possess to the poor and surrender my body to the flames, but have not love, I gain nothing.

Without love, our works are dead. We're just putting in time. Now, substitute the word "heart" for the word "love" in this passage. Take a look:

> If I speak in the tongues of men and of angels, but have *no heart*, I am only a resounding gong or a clanging cymbal. If I have the gift of prophecy and can fathom all mysteries and all knowledge, and if I have a faith that can move mountains, but have *no heart*, I am nothing. If I give all I possess to the poor and surrender my body to the flames, but have *no heart*, I gain nothing.

If our hearts aren't involved in our actions, then love is absent.

When you spend time with your children, are you just putting in time or are you giving them your heart? Do you say, "Hey son, I want to spend some time with you today. How about let's balance the checkbook together?" Or maybe you say to your daughter, "Hey honey, I thought about our day together and thought that we could clean out the file cabinet together." When we want to give to our children, we think about what they would like to do. We give them our hearts.

God wants our hearts as well. He wants heart and action. Dallas Willard writes, "Spiritual formation is no passive process. But Christlikeness of the inner being is not a human attainment. It is, finally a gift of grace."[7] To change our inner being takes action. But it isn't the action that changes our heart. God changes our heart through his gift of grace and that makes us more active people.

2 Corinthians 9:6-8 is usually used to speak about our financial contribution to the church, but perhaps we could use it here to speak of the heart and passivity. Paul writes:

> Remember this: Whoever sows sparingly will also reap sparingly, and whoever sows generously will also reap generously. Each man should give what he has decided in his heart to give, not reluctantly or under compulsion, for God loves a cheerful giver. And God is able to make all grace abound to you, so that in all things at all times, having all that you need, you will abound in every good work.

God wants us to sow generously. But he wants our generosity to be driven by intrinsic motivation and not extrinsic motivation.

The principle that Paul teaches here is: sow sparingly, reap sparingly; sow bountifully, reap bountifully. You can't sow bountifully unless your heart is in it. That is why God asks us to seek him with all our heart. "All the heart" is bountiful.

When we get our hearts right, we become more active for God. If you get your heart into anything, then you become active for it.

- Whether it's pulling for your favorite basketball team, or
- Reading your Bible, or
- Pulling for your favorite football team, or
- Praying to God, or
- Learning a new song on the guitar, or
- Sharing your faith with someone, or
- Spending time with your kids, or
- Singing a hymn to God, or
- Learning a new language, or
- Visiting the sick, or
- Working out, or
- Strengthening a weak disciple, or
- Finishing off that last room in your house, or
- Repenting of a sin, or
- Getting ready for a date with that special someone.

The way of the heart is not the way of passivity. If we go the way of the heart, then we will be more active for God than ever before. But the way of the heart is not action for action's sake. The way of the heart asks why we are doing something. Are we doing it to be seen by men or to glorify God? Is love behind our action? The active heart must know why it is doing what it is doing. The way of the heart is not the way of passivity. The way of the heart is the most active way of following God. It is action that is based upon God's grace and not our own human achievement.

Abba,

Protect my heart. Keep it safe. Be a refuge for my heart. Help me focus on things above and not on things below. Cleanse me of my sin and wrap me in new clothes of purity, love, faith, mercy and grace. Keep me safe in your arms. For you, O God, are my rock and my fortress. You are my protector. You are my sure and safe shelter in the raging storm.

In Jesus
Amen

Endnotes

1 Willard, *The Divine Conspiracy*, 80.

2 Theo Sorg, "Heart," in *The New International Dictionary of New Testament Theology*, Vol. II, Edited by Colin Brown (Grand Rapids: Zondervan Publishing House, 1976), 182.

3 N. T. Wright, *Colossians and Philemon,* Tyndale New Testament Commentaries (Grand Rapids: William B. Eerdmans Publishing Company, 1986),135.

4 Ibid, 136.

5 Foster, *Streams of Living Water*, 71.

6 Willard, *Renovation of the Heart*, 42.

7 Ibid, 24.

Part Two

What is the Way of the Heart

Christ as God is the homeland where we are going. Christ as man is the way we must travel.

–Augustine, church father

Today, we're enamored of the popular slogan "What would Jesus do?" Perhaps we'd be better off considering the question "What *did* Jesus do?"[1]

–Bruce Demarest, professor at Denver Seminary

We have now looked at what the Old Testament and the New Testament teach about the heart. Now that we have laid a solid Biblical foundation by defining how "heart" is used throughout the Bible, we can go on and study what it means to walk the way of the heart. We will see that walking the way of the heart is a continual process of subtraction and addition. We will also see that walking the way of the heart is a continual process of daily renewal. The next two chapters are entitled, The Disciples' Math: Subtraction and Addition, and The Disciples' Bath: Daily Inner Renewal.

Endnote

1 Bruce Demarest, *Soul Guide: Following Jesus as a Spiritual Director* (Colorado Springs: Navpress, 2003), 17.

Chapter Four

The Disciples' Math: Subtraction and Addition

The Fifth Psalm
To the chief Musician upon Nihility, a Psalm of David
–Paraphrased by the poet John Davies

Lord weigh my words, and take consideration
Of my sad thoughts, and silent meditation:
My God, my King, bow down thine ear to me,
While I send up mine humble prayer to thee.
Early before the morn doth bring the day
I will, O Lord, look up to thee and pray;
For thou with sin art never pleased well,
Nor any ill may with thy goodness dwell;
The fool may not before thy wisdom stand,
Nor shall the impious scape thy wrathful hand;
Thou wilt destroy all such as utter lies;
Blood and deceit are odious in thine eyes;
But trusting in thy many mercies dear,
I will approach thy house with holy fear.
Teach me thy plain and righteous way to go,
That I may never fall before my foe,
Whose flattering tongue is false, and heart impure,
And throat an open place of sepulture:
Destroy them Lord, and frustrate their devices,
Cast out those rebels for their many vices,
But all that trust in thee, and love thy name,
Make them rejoice, and rescue them from shame.
Thou wilt thy blessing to the righteous yield,
And guard them with thy grace as with a shield.[1]

The year 2003 was one of the worst years of my life. Our region of the church went through intense struggles. My family suffered through serious health problems. And I struggled with serious bouts of depression. I don't know if you've ever had times like that in your life, but I had never faced anything like what 2003 sent my way. I grew up in a happy home. I was always sheltered from the hurts of the world. I had never really had any extended times of sadness. 2003 changed all of that. I suffered through 2003. As the country preacher used to say, "I was lower than a snake's belly in a wagon's rut." As the year ended, I was ready for a new year. I didn't know what 2004 had in store, but I believed that it couldn't have been as bad as 2003. I did know a few things:

- God was still my Father;
- Jesus was still my Lord;
- The Spirit was still working for my good;
- I was still saved by the grace of God;
- The world was still lost without God;
- And the battle before me was a battle for my heart.

A friend of mine sent me an e-mail to lift my spirit. It read, "Think you're having a bad day, check out these actual cases." In fact, these were not actual cases, but urban legends.[2] However fictitious these modern-day fables turned out to be, reading them did inspire my gratitude.

Fire authorities in California found a corpse in a burned-out section of forest while assessing the damage done by a forest fire. The deceased male was dressed in a full wet suit, complete with scuba tanks on his back, flippers and a facemask.

A postmortem test revealed that the man died not from burns, but from massive internal injuries. Dental records provided a positive identification. Investigators then set about to determine how a fully clothed diver ended up in the middle of a forest fire. It was revealed that on the day of the fire, the man went diving off the coast, some 20 miles from the forest. The fire fighters, seeking to control the fire as quickly as possible, had called in a fleet of helicopters with very large dip buckets. Water was dipped from the ocean and emptied at the site of the forest fire.

You guessed it. One minute the diver was making like Flipper in the Pacific, the next, he was doing the breaststroke in a fire dip bucket 300 feet in the air. Some days it just doesn't pay to get out of bed.

Still think you're having a bad day? A man was working on his motorcycle on the patio, his wife nearby in the kitchen. While racing the engine, the motorcycle accidentally slipped into gear. The man, still holding onto the handlebars, was dragged along as it burst through the patio doors.

His wife, hearing the crash, ran in the room to find her husband cut and bleeding. She called for an ambulance and because the house sat on a fairly large hill, went down the several flights of stairs to meet the paramedics and escort them to her husband.

While the attendants were loading her husband, the wife managed to right the motorcycle and push it outside. She also quickly blotted up the spilled gasoline with some paper towels and tossed them into the toilet.

After being treated and released, the man returned home, looked at the shattered patio door and the damage done to his motorcycle. He went into the bathroom and consoled himself with a cigarette while attending to his business. About to stand, he flipped the butt between his legs. The wife, who was in the kitchen, heard a loud explosion and her husband screaming. Finding him lying on the bathroom floor with his trousers blown away and burns on his buttocks, legs and groin, she once again phoned for an ambulance. The same paramedic crew was dispatched.

As the paramedics carried the man down the stairs to the ambulance they asked the wife how he had come to burn himself. She told them. They stared laughing so hard that one slipped, dropping the stretcher and dumping the husband out. He fell down the remaining stairs, breaking his arm.

Still having a bad day? A woman came home to find her husband in the kitchen shaking frantically, almost in a dancing frenzy, with some kind of wire running from his waist towards the electric kettle. Intending to jolt him away from the deadly current, she whacked him with a handy plank of wood, breaking his arm in two places. Up to that moment, he had been happily listening to his Walkman.

2003 was a bad year for me. But all things considered, was it really that bad? Perhaps I should re-evaluate it with eyes of faith. I have been thinking about what my goals should be for my own life and for the life of the church in the future. I have decided to look at Paul and his desire for the disciples and the churches where he ministered. In Galatians 4:14 he writes to the church in Galatia saying, "My dear children, for whom I am again in the pains of childbirth until Christ is formed in you." Now that is a lofty goal. That is much more impressive than daily baptisms. That is more impressive than adding a dozen Bible study groups. That is more impressive than raising the contribution by $10,000. His goal was that Christ be formed in them. In other words, we must work on the heart. We must work on the internals and not the externals. Of course, if the internals are in place, then the externals will naturally follow. If Christ is formed in us, then we are going to share our faith with people and this will lead to baptisms. If Christ is formed in us, then we are going to sacrifice to the church and this will mean that the contribution will grow. But where we place our focus is important. If we focus on the results and not the heart, then we fail to walk the way of the heart.

What was Paul's prayer for the church in Ephesus? Paul writes to his brothers and sisters and says:

> For this reason I bow my knees before the Father, from whom every family in heaven and on earth takes its name. I pray that, according to the riches of his glory, he may grant that you may be strengthened in your inner being with power through his Spirit, and that Christ may dwell in your hearts through faith, as you are being rooted and grounded in love. I pray that you may have the power to comprehend, with all the saints, what is the breadth and length and height and depth, and to know the love of Christ that surpasses knowledge, so that you may be filled with all the fullness of God.
>
> Now to him who by the power at work within us is able to accomplish abundantly far more than all we can ask or imagine, to him be glory in the church and in Christ Jesus to all generations, forever and ever, Amen (Ephesians 3:14-21, NRSV).

Paul's prayer for the disciples here is that they might:

- Get strengthened in their inner being with power through the Spirit,
- So that Christ may dwell in their hearts through faith,
- That they would be rooted and established in love and grasp the love of Christ,
- That they would be filled to the measure of all the fullness of God.

All these ideas are about internals and not external. You can't place these on a stat sheet. Our focus must be in the right place. We must focus on Jesus and let him dwell in our hearts.

I have decided to spend the rest of my life focusing on the heart by walking the way of the heart. To do this I must renovate my heart. When you renovate something, be it your car, your apartment, your house, your business or your spiritual life, you have to take some things away and you have to add some things. To put up new cabinets in your kitchen, you have to get rid of the old cabinets to make room for the new. To renovate the heart means that I must take some things away and add some things. It takes subtraction and addition to renovate the heart.

When Paul describes the conversion process in Romans 6, he connects the conversion process with the death and resurrection of Jesus. Just as Jesus died and then rose from the dead, every disciple experiences death and resurrection when he or she is baptized. This image ties in perfectly with the image of subtraction and addition. Death is the subtraction; resurrection is the addition. At conversion we subtract or die to our old life of sin. Paul writes: "For we know that our old self was crucified with him so that the body of sin might be done away with, that we might be no longer be slaves to sin—because anyone who has died has been freed from sin" (Romans 6: 6-7). Subtract sin.

At conversion we add or are raised to live the new life in Christ. Paul writes, "We were therefore buried with him through baptism into death in order that, just as Christ was raised from the dead through the glory of the Father, we too may live a new life" (Romans 6:4). Add new life.

So the conversion process is a process of subtraction and addition. But the process of subtraction and addition does not end at conversion. Conversion is only the beginning of the process. Our walk as apprentices of Jesus is a walk where we are constantly subtracting and adding qualities to our lives.

Subtraction:

For the grace of God has appeared for the salvation of all men, training us to renounce irreligion and worldly passions, and to live sober, upright, and godly lives in this world, awaiting our blessed hope, the appearing of the glory of our great God and Savior Jesus Christ, who gave himself for us to redeem us from all iniquity and to purify for himself a people of his own who are zealous for good deeds (Titus 2:11-12, RSV).

The acts of the sinful nature are obvious: sexual immorality, impurity and debauchery; idolatry and witchcraft; hatred, discord, jealousy, fits of rage, selfish ambition, dissensions, factions and envy; drunkenness, orgies, and the like. I warn you, as I did before, that those who live like this will not inherit the kingdom of God (Galatians 5:19-21).

Addition:

But the fruit of the Spirit is love, joy, peace, patience, kindness, goodness, faithfulness, gentleness and self-control. Against such things there is no law. Those who belong to Christ Jesus have crucified the sinful nature with its passions and desires. Since we live by the Spirit, let us keep in step with the Spirit (Galatians 5:22-25).

His divine power has granted to us all things that pertain to life and godliness, through the knowledge of him who called us to his own glory and excellence, by which he has granted to us his precious and very great promises, that through these you may escape from the corruption that is in the world because of passion, and become partakers of the divine nature.

For this very reason make every effort to supplement your faith with virtue, and virtue with knowledge, and knowledge with self-control, and self-control with steadfastness, and steadfastness with godliness, and godliness with brotherly affection, and brotherly affection with love. For if these things are yours and abound, they keep you from being ineffective or unfruitful in the knowledge of our Lord Jesus Christ. For

> whoever lacks these things is blind and shortsighted and has forgotten that he was cleansed from his old sins.
>
> Therefore, brethren, be the more zealous to confirm your call and election, for if you do this you will never fall; so there will be richly provided for you an entrance into the eternal kingdom of our Lord and Savior Jesus Christ. Therefore I intend always to remind you of these things, though you know them and are established in the truth that you have (2 Peter 1: 3-12, RSV).

This is the way of the heart. It is the path of subtraction and addition. We subtract the flesh and add the spirit. We subtract impurity and add purity. We subtract debauchery and add self-control. We subtract hatred and add love. We subtract fits of rage and add patience. We subtract selfish ambition and add selflessness. We subtract evil thoughts and add good thoughts. We subtract deceit and add honesty. We subtract arrogance and add humility. What do you need to subtract and add to your life?

My hands were filled with many things
That I did precious hold,
As any treasure of a king's—
Silver, or gems, or gold.
The Master came and *touched* my hands,
(The scars were in His own)
And at His feet my treasures sweet
Fell shattered, one by one.
"I must have empty hands," said He,
"Wherewith to work My works through thee."

My hands were stained with marks of toil,
Defiled with dust of earth;
And I my work did ofttimes soil,
And render little worth.
The Master came and *touched* my hands,
(And crimson were His own)
But when, amazed, on mine I gazed,
Lo! Every stain was gone.
"I must have cleansed hands," said He,
"Wherewith to work My works through thee."

My hands were growing feverish
And cumbered with much care!
Trembling with haste and eagerness,
Nor folded oft in prayer.
The Master came and *touched* my hands,
(With healing in his own)
And calm and still to do His will
They grew—the fever gone.
"I must have quiet hands," said He,
"Wherewith to work My works for Me."

My hands were strong in fancied strength,
But not in power divine,
And bold to take up tasks at length,
That were not His but mine.
The Master came and *touched* my hands,
(and might was in His own!)
But mine since then have powerless been,
Save His are laid thereon.
"And it is only thus," said He,
"That I can work my works through thee."[3]

–S. D. Gordon

Father,

I desperately need Christ formed in me. Give me the heart of Jesus. Help me to subtract from my life anything that will keep me from becoming like Jesus. Add to my life anything that will transform me into the image of your Son.

In His name

Amen

Endnotes

1 *The Poets' Book of Psalms.* Compiled and edited by Laurance Wieder (San Francisco: HarperSanFrancisco, 1991), 10.

2 These stories have been recorded by Ahmad Anvari and were found at http://www.anvari.org/fun/Trth/Having_a_Bad_Day.html (accessed March 22, 2006).

3 S.D. Gordon, *Quiet Talks on Power* (London: Fleming H. Revell Company, 1903), 56-57.

Chapter Five

The Disciples' Bath: Daily Inner Renewal

> Therefore, we do not lose heart. Though outwardly we are wasting away, yet inwardly we are being renewed day by day. For our light and momentary troubles are achieving for us an eternal glory that outweighs them all. So we fix our eyes not on what is seen, but on what is unseen. For what is seen is temporary, but what is unseen is eternal.
>
> (2 Corinthians 4:16-18)

We've looked at the disciples' math: subtraction and addition. Now let's look at the disciples' bath: inner renewal. Cleanliness is next to godliness, according to the ancient proverb. But God isn't as concerned with our outward cleanliness as he is with our inward cleanliness. When Peter speaks of the act of baptism, he says that it is "not the removal of dirt from the body but the pledge of a good conscience toward God" (1 Peter 3:21). Baptism doesn't cleanse our body, but it does cleanse our soul. Baptism isn't an outer bath; it is an inner bath. But just because we clean the inner person at baptism, doesn't mean that we don't need to keep cleaning the inner person. To be an apprentice of Jesus, we must constantly clean the inside. This is the way of the heart. It is about keeping the inside of the cup clean. In 2 Corinthians 4:16-18 Paul speaks of our inward renewal. What does it mean to become new from the inside out? Let's see what Paul says about this concept in this passage.

"We do not lose heart."

Paul begins with a simple statement, "We do not lose heart." Have you ever set a goal, but you didn't complete the goal? This has happened to me several times, actually, more times than I wish to confess in this book. Most recently it happened with a decision I made to keep our basement uncluttered. I spent the day and cleaned the basement from top to bottom. I put everything away so that you could actually walk across the floor without tripping on anything. This was great accomplishment. I felt so proud that the basement was perfectly clean. But then, I took some things off the shelves and didn't put them back in place. My daughter cleaned out her room and put some of her old stuff on the basement floor. A few days later, my wife put some things that she didn't want upstairs in the basement. Before I knew it, the basement was just as cluttered as it had been before I cleaned it. I lost heart, and the basement became cluttered.

It is easy to lose heart. Whether you are talking about keeping your room clean, working on a project at school, staying close to a friend or staying on a diet; it is easy to lose heart. The same is true in our relationship with God. We can easily lose heart. We start out with great energy. Things seem to flow easily. Then we hit some bumps. We don't make time for Bible study or prayer. People disappoint us. We lose heart.

In J. R. R. Tolkien's *The Lord of the Rings*[1], Frodo Baggins is chosen to carry the ring of power into Mordor in order to destroy it. Frodo knows that the ring must be destroyed. It is either destroy the ring or the ring will destroy Middle Earth. He begins the journey with great determination. But along the way, the ring begins to weigh on him. He begins to struggle with his motives. He questions his allegiance. He begins to lose heart. He wants to give into the power of the ring.

His traveling companion, Sam Gamgee, has to remind Frodo of the quest. He reminds him of the Shire and what they are fighting for. He reminds him of the good things back home. He strengthens him.

Sam had his own struggles. But he was a good friend to Frodo. We need friends who will remind us not to lose heart. I'm thankful for friends like that. Thankful for my wife, Leigh. Thankful for my daughter, Chelsea and my son, Daniel. For my fellow evangelists in New York, Sam Powell and Shane Engle. For my elders. For friends like Phil Garrison, Phil Zayas, Matt Fridley and C. Mack. These guys are my "peeps." They encourage me. They keep me from losing heart. They are my Sam Gamgee. We all need some people in our lives that will keep us from losing heart.

"Outwardly we are wasting away."

The word "outwardly" can also be translated as "the external."[2] The words "wasting away" can also be translated as "to rot or to decay." "Wasting away" is in the present tense signifying a continual process of decay. So we could translate this phrase as "the externals continually destroy us." When we focus on the externals, we rot away. When we focus on the internals, we can be renewed.

But this verse also shows us how the external forces in our lives are always battling with our spirit in hopes of destroying our spirit. What are some of these outside forces that work on our hearts?

- Home environment
- The world around us
- School surroundings
- Church community
- Personal choices
- Genetic makeup
- Friendships
- Workplace
- Weaknesses
- Fears
- Persecution

Let's not let the externals continually destroy us. Instead, let's allow God to renew us day by day.

"Inwardly, we are being renewed day by day."

"Inwardly" can also be translated as "the internals." The word "renewed" is in the present tense denoting a continual process. The internals keep us constantly renewed. "Day by day" can also be translated as "daily." So we could translate this phrase as "the internals continually renew us every day." To not lose heart, we must experience daily renewal. The way of the heart is a matter of daily inner renewal. To be renewed, we must focus on the internals.

Which motivates you more, to go out and meet ten people because it is required of you or to share your faith with one person because your heart prompts you to share? Which gives you more satisfaction, to drop a check in the plate each week because you've filled out a pledge card and you must fulfill your commitment or to contribute your money because your heart is moved by compassion over the hurt of the world?

We must decide if we are going to let our heart be formed by outside forces or if we are going to renew our hearts day by day. Do you know how a petrified tree becomes a petrified tree? It was once a living organism with healthy living tissue. Then it falls and is covered by sediment. Over time, calcite and silicon enter the cells of the tree and take the shape of the tree cells. The tree becomes calcified. It becomes rock. It is no longer a tree. It looks like a tree. But it is stone.

The same thing can happen to our hearts. It doesn't happen over night. It happens over time. We allow the external forces of the world to steal our joy, our enthusiasm, our love for life, our faith—and over time our hearts become stone. They become calcified.

We must guard against a hard, calcified heart. Hebrews 3:7-8 reads, "So, as the Holy Spirit says, 'Today, if you hear his voice, do not harden your hearts as you did in the rebellion, during the time of testing in the dcsert.'" This same thought is repeated in verse 15. Why repeat the same thought so soon? Because, this was a real temptation for the early disciples. And it is a real temptation for us as well. We must not allow our hearts to calcify.

Hebrews 4:7 reads, "Therefore God again set a certain day, calling it Today, when a long time later he spoke through David, as was said, before: 'Today, if you hear his voice, do not harden your hearts.'" Here it is again. The same warning—do not harden your hearts. How do we protect against calcification of the heart? We must renew our hearts every single day. Daily inner cleansing is how to keep the heart soft. Dallas Willard writes:

> The greatest need you and I have—the greatest need of collective humanity—is renovation of the heart. That spiritual place within us from which outlook, choices, and actions come has been formed by a world away from God. Now it must be transformed.[3]

To be transformed, we must let go of the externals and cling to the internals.

"Our light and momentary troubles are achieving for us an eternal glory."

We must face the troubles in life with faith and not fear. Philip Yancey in *Rumors of Another World* writes:

> Do not be afraid is the most frequent command in the Bible, which seems wholly appropriate in an age when terrorists could strike at any moment and a mailed envelope may carry a biological agent. We have a thousand fears; mammograms and prostate tests, our children's future as well as their present, retirement funds, job security, crime. We fear not getting the job we want or the girlfriend/boyfriend we desire, and if we have them we fear their loss. In face of such everyday fear, Jesus points to a lily, or a sparrow, and calmly says, "Trust." Seek first the kingdom of heaven.[4]

When we are in the midst of our troubles, they seem anything but "light and momentary." It is only when we can step back from the struggle and compare it to the eternal glory that God gives that we get perspective. The struggles are getting us ready to receive the eternal glory of God. Dr. Larry Crabb, in his excellent book entitled *Inside-Out*, writes:

> The true nature of spiritual growth, assumes a key principle: Until we acknowledge painful disappointment in our circumstances and relationships (particularly the latter), we will not pursue Christ with the passion of a deep thirst. Or, to put it more simply, we rarely learn to meaningfully depend on God when our lives are comfortable.[5]

Therefore, we must not lose heart. We must push through the struggle and come out on the other side. When we are on the other side of the side of the struggle, then we can see the lessons that we learned. Through this experience, we are able to help other people, and this brings glory to God.

"Fix our eyes not on what is seen but on what is unseen."

We live in an age of instant gratification. We live in an age where we want what we want, when we want it. We have no time to wait. We fix our eyes on what we see, and we grab it. Consider the following:

- Fast food
- Cell phones
- High speed modems
- Pay per view movies
- ATM's on every corner
- Express mail
- TiVo[6]
- Microwave ovens

But the world of the eternal isn't about grabbing what you see in front of you. The eternal world (the spiritual realm) is about patiently waiting for things that aren't there. It is about visualizing the invisible. It is about feeding the spirit and not the flesh. Paul writes in Romans 8:5-8:

> Those who live according to the sinful nature have their minds set on what that nature desires; but those who live in accordance with the Spirit have their minds set on what the Spirit desires. The mind of sinful man is death, but the mind controlled by the Spirit is life and peace; the sinful mind is hostile to God. It does not submit to God's law, nor can it do so. Those controlled by the sinful nature cannot please God.

In the words of the Pixies, ask yourself, "Where is my mind?"[6] Are you thinking about the spiritual realm or the physical world? To not lose heart, we need to keep our minds focused on the spiritual world. We must enter the divine realm. Dallas Willard writes, "The perceived distance and difficulty of entering fully into the divine world and its life is due entirely to our failure to understand that the way in is the way of pervasive and inner transformation and to our failure to take small steps that quietly and certainly lead to it."[7] So to enter the divine realm, we must transform our hearts. And to transform our hearts, we must enter the divine realm. This is the yin and the yang of walking the way of the heart.

Moving from a performance-based religiosity to a dependence-based spirituality.

God doesn't want us to perform. He's not looking to hand out Academy Awards. God wants us to be genuine. He wants us to learn how to depend on him.

Throughout history, religion has brought out the tendency in people to perform religious acts without their heart being invested in those acts. This is performance-based religiosity. God wants us to move away from a performance-based religiosity toward a dependence-based spirituality. In a dependence-based spirituality our hearts are engaged. We learn to depend on God to move our hearts. Our actions flow from proper motivation.

Religious acts are such that if we are not careful they can become performance-based instead of heart-based. Do you worship God with the same fervor when you are by yourself versus when you think someone might be watching you? Are your prayers just as heartfelt when you are praying alone as they are when you are asked to lead a prayer before a group? Are you more inclined to serve if you think that another person will notice your service? We have to be able to see behind our actions to the motivation of our heart.

In his book *Inside Out*, Dr. Crabb uses the illustration of an iceberg to demonstrate what we can easily see in our behavior versus what is not easily seen in our motives.[8] In a similar way, you can use the analogy of a tree to show the difference between performance-based religiosity and dependence-based spirituality.

When we look at a tree, we see what is above ground. We see the trunk, the branches and the foliage. We see the attractive flowers and the fruit in season. We might see some of the roots that are above ground, but we are mostly unaware of what is unseen. Yet it is the roots that feed the tree and have a tremendous impact on the health of what we can see. In some species, the root system is as large as or even larger below ground than the rest of the tree is above ground.

What we see each other doing in and around church is what is above ground—our actions, our performance and even our feelings. What remains unseen below ground is what lies behind the action—our motives, our attitudes and our urges. To make what is above the ground meaningful, we have to work on the things that lie below.

Where do we place most of our focus? It is usually on the matters that are aboveground—actions, thoughts and feeling. But the ideas that are below, the ideas that get less of our focus, are actually more crucial when it comes to walking the way of the heart. If we work on things belowground, then the things above will naturally be affected. Think dependence and not performance. Think dependence-based spirituality and not performance-based religiosity.

Dear Abba,

Help me depend on you. I don't want to be a performer. I've been a performer for too long. I genuinely want to depend on you. Help me to let go of the externals and to cling to the internals. Help me not to run from trouble but allow me to learn the lessons that you want to teach me through every tough life situation. And Abba, help me to fix my eyes not on what is seen, but on what cannot be seen with the eye. Help me to see the eternal. Form Christ in me.

In Jesus' name
Amen

Endnotes

[1] J. R. R. Tolkien, *The Lord of the Rings*, Second Edition (Boston: Houghton Mifflin Company Boston), 1965.

[2] Reinecker, 465.

[3] Willard, *Renovation of the Heart*, 14.

[4] Philip Yancey, *Rumors of Another World: What on Earth Are We Missing?* (Grand Rapids: Zondervan, 2003), 217.

[5] Larry Crabb, *Inside-Out* (Colorado Springs: NavPress, 1988), 87.

[6] The Pixies, "Where Is My Mind?" *Death to the Pixies*, written by Black Francies, published by Rice and Beans Music. 4 A.D. 1988.

[7] I consider TiVo the greatest invention since the internal combustion engine.

[8] Willard, *Renovation of the Heart*, 10.

[9] Crabb, 44.

Part Three

The Heart of the Trinity

> God's triunity is not only the summit of the task of theology, it is absolutely foundational for the very living of the Christian life in devotion, in witness, in consecration.... The Father is depth because of his unfathomable love for the Son, the Son is the visualization and representation of the Father's mystery, and the Holy Spirit is the One through whom the Father speaks his Word eternally.[1]
>
> –Roderick T. Leupp, professor of theology

The Trinity is an important theological concept. The Trinity teaches us about the relational aspect of God. Our God is one. But our God is also Father, Son and Holy Spirit. The Father, Son and Holy Spirit are continually connected to each other. They have always been connected and will always stay connected. Connected together for eternity. Together they make the Triune God. The heart of the Trinity is a relational heart.

In this section we are going to take a closer look at the heart of the Trinity by taking a closer look at the heart of the Father, the heart of the Son and the heart of the Holy Spirit. By looking at the heart of the Father, the heart of the Son and the heart of the Holy Spirit, we can learn about the relational, connected heart of the Triune God.

Endnotes

[1] Roderick T. Leupp, *Knowing the Name of God: A Trinitarian Tapestry of Grace, Faith and Community* (Downers Grove: Intervarsity Press, 1996), 13-14.

Chapter Six

The Heart of the Father

> The most enjoyable of all subjects has to be God, because God is the source of all joy. God has the first and last laugh.[1]
>
> –Thomas C. Oden, professor of theology

What is the heart of God the Father? When we ask this question, we are asking, who is the Father? We cannot separate God from his nature. The heart of the Father is the character of the Father. His heart is who he is.

We ask this question because we want to know him and to be like him. This presupposes that we believe in God's existence and that we believe that he can be known (epistemology).

I believe in God not because of some elaborate argument for his existence (teleological, cosmological, moral or ontological). I believe because I have experienced his existence.

We can gain knowledge of the Father in many ways:

- through creation
- through his Word
- through his Son
- through his Spirit
- through experience
- through the church
- through family and friends
- through suffering
- through prayer
- through meditation

I first learned about God through a big, thick Bible story picture book that my Mom and Dad read to me at night. I then learned about God in Sunday School and Wednesday night classes at the Graymere Church of Christ in Columbia, Tennessee. I then learned about God through nature while I was a Boy Scout. I then experienced God through my conversion. Since then I have experienced God by walking in his Spirit. My brothers and sisters in the fellowship have taught me about God. My wife and children have taught me about God. My dog, Sunshine, has taught me about God. My personal suffering has taught me about God. God is everywhere. He can be experienced in various ways. I need to keep my spiritual sensors in tune so that I can learn lessons about God through the many experiences that he sends my way every single day.

The Names of God

> Is there any God beside me? (Isaiah 44:8).

In the Hebrew tradition names were thought to reveal the character of a person. They were believed to convey some aspect of his or her nature. The Bible gives many names for God. Each name reveals something about God's character. Here are some of the names of God. In parenthesis is a translation of what the name means:[2]

- *Yahweh* (He Who Is, The "Ising" One, Mr. Is) Genesis 2:4-9, Exodus 3:13-14, Psalm 23:1, Isaiah 6:3.
- *El* (Strong and Mighty One) Genesis 14:18-ff, Psalm 90:2.
- *El Shaddai* (God Almighty, The All-Sufficient God) Genesis 28:3.
- *El Elyon* (God Most High).
- *El Olam* (The Everlasting God) Romans 16:26.
- *Yahweh Sabaoth* (Lord of Hosts, Lord of the Angel Armies) Psalm 46:7.
- *Adonai* (Lord) Psalm 38:22.
- *Chai Elohim* (God is the Living, Present God) 1 Samuel 17:26; Psalm 42:2.

The names of God demonstrate that God has personhood. He is not an abstract idea, a nameless energy. He is not an "it." Therefore, we can have a relationship with him. The Scriptures speak of meeting God, listening to him, speaking to him, getting acquainted with him and experiencing him.

God has both intellect and emotion. The scriptures reveal that God repents (Genesis 6:6) and gets angry (Deuteronomy 1:37). God is full of love and compassion. Our God is a jealous God (Exodus 20: 5). Only a personal being can have these emotions. God is not just an idea; he is a person.

Who is God?

> At times God is quietly present, at other times actively; at times hiddenly, at other times revealed.[3]
>
> –Thomas C. Oden, professor of theology

> The God who called the world into being loves us and cares for us—coming down from heaven and going to the cross to prove the full extent of that love to a disbelieving and wondering world.[4]
>
> –Alister McGrath, spiritual author

Who is God? The Bible tells us that God is Spirit (John 4:24), God is holy (Isaiah 6:1-10) and God is love (1 John 4:16-18). But the Bible also gives us images to help us understand the heart of God. Let's look at four biblical images that teach us about the nature of God the Father.

God as Shepherd

Isaiah 40:10-11says:

> See, the Sovereign Lord comes with power,
> and his arm rules for him.
> See, his reward is with him,
> and his recompense accompanies him.
> He tends his flock like a shepherd:
> He gathers the lambs in his arms
> and carries them close to his heart;
> he gently leads those that have young.

What are some of the characteristics of a shepherd?

- The shepherd takes care of the sheep.
- The sheep know the shepherd, and they listen to his voice.
- He calls his sheep by name. He knows them individually.
- He walks ahead of his sheep, and they follow him. He leads them.
- He lays down his life for the sheep. He will put himself in harm's way to take care of the sheep.

When my family lived in Jerusalem, I became friends with the family that owned the kiosk at the gate of Hezekiah's Tunnel. They would let us into the tunnel whenever we wanted. Every now and then I would have supper with them. Some of my fondest memories from our days in Jerusalem come from sitting in front of Hezekiah's Tunnel visiting with this Arab family. One evening as we were sitting down for dinner, a man came strolling up to our table with a staff in his hand. The family welcomed him. He joined us for dinner. About half a minute after he arrived, I heard the sound of sheep from around the corner. A few seconds later twenty to thirty sheep came. This was his flock of sheep. He was a shepherd by trade. That was his full-time profession. The sheep followed their shepherd wherever he led them. Tonight he had led them to our supper table. It was the first night I had ever had supper with a shepherd and his flock of sheep.

I talked to the shepherd about his sheep. He taught me many lessons about sheep. He told me how vulnerable they were. He had to keep watch over them all the time. He had to bring them in from the cold and protect them from the elements.

I asked him if he knew them all by name, and he said that he did. He was with them all the time. He never went anywhere without his sheep. They were his life.

God is our shepherd. He watches over us as a shepherd watches over his sheep. He protects us, keeps us safe, knows us by name, cares for us, meets our every need and leads us to green pasture.

Do you ever feel insecure? Do you ever feel fearful about life? Do you ever wonder about your future? I know that I struggle with these thoughts. When we are bombarded by these thoughts, we need to stop and say, "The Lord is my shepherd." God is always with us. He will never leave us alone. Even when the hour seems the darkest, God is with us leading us to a green pasture. We need to place our confidence in God as a shepherd because he cares for his sheep.

God as Parent

Jesus refers to God as Father (Abba). The Lord's Prayer begins, "Our Father who is in heaven." Notice Jesus says "our" Father, and not "my" Father. In doing so, he teaches us to look at God as our Father. God cares for us as a father cares for his children. But for many people, to use the image of God as father isn't a helpful image.

For many people they would rather forget their memories of their father. Their father beat or abused them. Their father left them when they were young. They never knew their father. They can't conjure up a healthy image of a father.

But I was one of the lucky ones who had a great father when I was growing up. So, for me, the image of God as a loving father is a healthy image that I find very comforting. My father provided for our family. He worked long, hard hours to make sure that we had food on the table, clothes on our back and a roof over our heads. He spent what little extra time he had teaching me how to throw a football or how to strike a golf ball. He taught me about our heavenly Father. This is the image that God wants us to have when we think of him as father.

Consider the 15th chapter of Luke. I call this the "lost chapter." In this chapter Jesus tells three parables—the parable of the lost sheep, the parable of the lost coin and the parable of the lost son. In the third parable, the parable of the lost son, God is compared to a father who allows his son to leave home with his inheritance. The son wastes all his money in wild, reckless living. When he has nothing left to live on, he returns home to his father. The father is there to welcome him back and to pick up the pieces. The father shows mercy and grace to his son. The father accepts the son back home without any penalty or any punishment.

In this parable, God is the father, and we are the son. No matter how far we stray away from God, God is faithful. He will always be there to accept us back home. My own earthly father was this way with me. I have often made mistakes in my life. I have often made decisions that he would not personally have made. But through all those decisions, my father always let me know that he believed in me, that he trusted me and that he was proud to be my father.

No matter how badly you have messed up. No matter how terribly you have sinned. No matter how low you feel. No matter how disgusted you are with yourself. No matter how far you have strayed from home. Realize that God is a gracious, loving father who stands looking out the window awaiting your return. Don't be afraid to return home. God is ready to receive you with open arms.

God loves us as a loving father. His love should fill us with confidence. It should strengthen our self-worth. The creator of the universe is our Dad. He is our Abba. The heart of God is the heart of a loving father.

God as Defender of Orphans

The helpless put their trust in you. You are the defender of orphans (Psalm 10:14).

You hear, O Lord, the desire of the afflicted, you strengthen their heart, you listen to them and defend the orphans and the helpless, so that man, who is of the earth, may terrify no more (Psalm 10:17-18).

But I will strip Esau bare;
I will uncover his hiding places,
So that he cannot conceal himself.
His children, relatives and neighbors
Will perish, And he will be no more.
Leave your orphans; I will protect their lives.
Your widows too can trust in me (Jeremiah 49:10-11).

Defend the cause of the weak and fatherless;
    Maintain the rights of the poor and oppressed.
Rescue the weak and needy;
    Deliver them from the hand of the wicked.
They know nothing, they understand nothing.
    They walk about in darkness;
All the foundations of the earth are shaken (Psalm 82:3-5).

I love comic books and comic book heroes. Comic book heroes defend the rights of the helpless. They come to rescue people who cannot fend for themselves. I'm sure that each of us would like to have little comic book hero in us. We want to right wrongs and help the helpless. We want to fight injustice.

Comic book heroes are fictional characters. God is a true superhero. He is the defender of orphans. He comes to their aid in their most desperate time of need. This is the heart of God.

Growing up, I didn't know many orphans. All the kids that I grew up with had a mom and a dad. The town next to us had an orphans' home that was run by the Churches of Christ. Whenever we drove by it, it always had a cold, institutional look to it. I never saw the kids playing outside in the playground. I often wondered what the conditions were like inside the orphanage. But to my shame, I never visited to see what it was like or to reach out to the children who lived there.

But when my family lived in the Holy Lands, we got to know some orphans. They lived in the Four Homes of Mercy in Bethany. The Palestinians ran this home, and the children who stayed there were Arab. Most of the children suffered severe mental and physical handicaps. Most of them couldn't speak. Many of them had some type of physical deformity.

The Four Homes of Mercy had very limited resources for the care of their patients. They had a great need for volunteers. On Saturdays most of our church members would go to the Four Homes of Mercy to reach out to the patients there. We would help feed them lunch. We would have parties and play games. We also painted the walls of the facility in bright murals of landscapes and seacoasts and flowers and animals. We were just trying to help lift the spirits of the children.

I remember one boy who was severely retarded and had very little control of his arms or legs. We would sit with him in a pile of balls and throw the balls up in the air all around us. He would watch the balls go up and down and bounce all around him. And when he did, he would laugh and laugh and laugh. I believe that when he laughed like that, God was laughing along with him. I believe this because I know that God holds the interests and concern of the orphan, the weak, the needy and the helpless deep in his heart. This is who God is. This is the heart of the Father.

God is the defender of orphans. He is their superhero. I believe that God was with us in our work in the Four Homes of Mercy in Bethany. I believe that God is always present when we reach out and help the helpless.

God as Worry Catcher

Do you know what a dream-catcher is? You've probably seen one in a shop that sells Native American items. A dream-catcher is a circle that is covered with yarn. Inside the circle, string is stretched from one side to the other forming a geometric design that looks like a spider web. You are to hang a dream-catcher above the place where you sleep. Native Americans believe that the dream-catcher acts as a sieve to allow good dreams to come into your mind while trapping the nightmares before they reach your mind. This is a wonderful concept. I wished it worked.

Wouldn't it be great if we could do something like this for worry? What if we could develop a worry-catcher—a device that would catch all our worries before they entered our mind? We could place this device in our shirt pocket and walk around with confidence knowing that as long as we had the worry-catcher close to our heart that no worry could overcome us. What a great concept! Perhaps I should market it.

God wants to be our worry-catcher. He implores us to "give all your worries to him, because he 'worries' for you" (1 Peter 5:7). The Psalmist writes, "I sing to the Lord because he has taken care of me" (Psalm 13:6). Again, the Psalmist says, "Give your worries to the Lord, and he will take care of you. He will never let the righteous fall" (Psalm 55:22). God doesn't want us to worry. And when we do worry, he wants us to cast our worries and concerns on him. He wants to be our worry-catcher.

I have always been the kind of person who worries. I have a nervous stomach that really acts up when I become anxious. My father is that way, and I guess I get it from him. But it wasn't until my mid-forties that I had my first full-blown panic attack. I started to hyperventilate. My pulse quickened, and my heart rate shot up. I felt like my heart was going to leap out of my chest. I got dizzy and disoriented. I fell facedown on the floor and started gasping for air. My face began to sweat. My stomach felt empty. I felt like I was going to pass out. I felt like I was having a heart attack. But inside I knew that it wasn't a heart attack; it was a panic attack.

As I laid on the floor, I began to pray. I prayed that God would ease my spirit and take away my worries. In order to slow down my heart rate, I took long, slow, even breaths. I meditated on each breath. I focused on breathing in blessings from God, and then I exhaled the frantic, anxious thoughts that I was feeling. I pictured myself standing under a waterfall of God's mercy. In time, my anxious thoughts began to subside. My heart rate and pulse went back to normal. I gave my cares and worries to God, and he took care of me.

That isn't the only time I've had a panic attack. I've experienced others since that first one. Whenever I feel my pulse quicken and my heartbeat start to race, I begin to slow down my breathing and focus on breathing in the blessings of God and breathing out my worries and frustrations. God helps me through those times. He helps me because he is my worry-catcher. That is his heart. He wants me to cast all my cares and anxiety on him, because he cares for me. Allow God to be your worry-catcher.

Abba,

Thank you for being my Abba. Thank you for being the shepherd of my soul who watches out for my well-being every hour, minute and second of every single day. Thank you for being a loving parent who always welcomes me back home. Thank you for being the true superhero who defends the orphan, the helpless, the hapless and the hopeless. Thank you for allowing me to cast all my cares and worries on you. Abba, you are my worry-catcher.

In the name of your Son, Jesus
Amen

Endnotes

1 Thomas C. Oden, *The Living God, Systematic Theology: Volume One* (San Francisco: Harper San Francisco, 1992).

2 Some of this material follows the outline from Oden's *The Living God*, 32-34.

3 Oden, *The Living God*, 69.

4 Alister McGrath, *The Unknown God: Searching for Spiritual Fulfillment* (Grand Rapids: Eerdmans, 1999), 111.

Chapter Seven

The Heart of the Son

The real Son of God is at your side. He is beginning to turn you into the same kind of thing as Himself. He is beginning, so to speak, to "inject"" His kind of life and thought, His *Zoe* [life], into you; beginning to turn the tin soldier into a live man. The part of you that does not like it is the part that is still tin.[1]

–C. S. Lewis, spiritual author

At the literally mundane level, Jesus knew how to transform the molecular structure of water to make it wine. That knowledge also allowed him to take a few pieces of bread and some little fish and feed thousands of people. He could create matter from the energy he knew how to access from 'the heavens,' right where he was.

It cannot be surprising that the feeding of the thousands led the crowds to try to force him to be their king. Surely one who could play on the energy/matter equation like that could do anything. Turn gravel into gold and pay off the national debt! Do you think he could get elected president or prime minister today?

He knew how to transform the tissues of the human body from sickness to health and from death to life. He knew how to suspend gravity, interrupt weather patterns, and eliminate unfruitful trees without saw or ax. He only needed a word. Surely he must be amused at what Nobel prizes are awarded for today.[2]

–Dallas Willard, spiritual writer and theologian

The Incarnation: Jesus Took on Our Skin.

God has come to us in a human word, and his name is Jesus Christ. The *kabod Yahweh* [glory of the Lord],[3] which frightens us out of all sense of security, speaks to us in human language, and the word *love* is no longer anything we must fear.

> When Jesus says, "As the Father has loved me, so I have loved you. Live on in my love" (John 15:9), this word comes from a human heart. While his love is incomparably greater than our human love, because his heart is the heart of God, it is still love and becomes in a limited way comprehensible to our feeble understanding.[4]
>
> –Brennan Manning, spiritual writer

> The results of the incarnation of the Savior are such and so many, that anyone attempting to enumerate them should be compared to a person looking upon the vastness of the sea and attempting to count its waves.
>
> –Athanasius (295-373 CE), early church father

I heard a story about a four-year-old girl who woke up one night really frightened believing there were monsters and ghosts in her room. She walked down the hall and got her mom. Her mom took her back to her room, turned on the light, opened the closet door, looked under the bed and assured her daughter that there was nothing to be afraid of.

She told her daughter, "Honey, there are no monsters here. There are no ghosts here."

Her daughter looked up at her mom and replied, "But I don't want to be alone."

The mother responded, "You're not alone. God is here in this room with you."

Her daughter then said, "I know God is here. But I need someone in this room who has some skin."

God must have felt this way about us. He must have felt that we needed someone with some skin. So he sent Jesus into the world. Jesus was God with skin. He was God in the flesh. This is the literal meaning of *incarnation*. God took on skin for us.

The Beloved Apostle writes:

> What was from the beginning, what we have heard, what we have seen with our eyes, what we have looked at and touched with our hands, concerning the Word of Life—and the life was manifested, and we have seen and testify and proclaim to you the eternal life, which was with the Father and was manifested to us—what we have seen and heard we proclaim to you also,

so that you too may have fellowship with us; and indeed our fellowship is with the Father, and with his Son Jesus Christ. These things we write, so that our joy may be made complete (1 John 1:1-4, NASV).

The writer of the Letter to the Hebrews states:

> Therefore, since we have a great high priest who has passed through the heavens, Jesus the Son of God, let us hold fast our confession. For we do not have a high priest who cannot sympathize with our weaknesses, but One who has been tempted in all things as we are, yet without sin. Therefore let us draw near with confidence to the throne of grace, so that we may receive mercy and find grace to help in time of need (Hebrews 4:14-16, NASV).

Since God took on skin, he has experienced everything that we experience. Before the incarnation, God already empathized with us. But since he came to the earth, we can visualize his empathy. We can feel more of a connection with him. We know him better. John 1: 14 says, "The Word became flesh and made his dwelling among us." *The Message* translates this as, "The Word became flesh and blood and moved into the neighborhood. We saw the glory with our own eyes."[5] The incarnation of Jesus allows us to feel a closer connection with God.

But you could protest, "The incarnation happened a long time ago." You could say, "But Jesus hasn't walked the earth in some 2,000 years." Today we could still say to God, "We need some skin." Where do we see God becoming flesh today? We see God in the flesh by looking at the church. Ephesians 5:23 reads, "Christ is the head of the church. His body, of which he is Savior." Peter Scazzero, author of *The Emotionally Healthy Church,* writes:

> Today, God still has physical skin and can be seen, touched, heard, and tasted. How? Through his body, the church, in whom he dwells. We are called, in the name of Jesus and by the indwelling Holy Spirit, to be skin for people all around us.[6]

Just as Jesus took on our skin, we, the church, take on his skin and become the incarnation of Jesus for people around us.

Those of us in the church are called to be the skin of Jesus. Have no doubt; people want to see Jesus in the flesh.

I'm thankful for people who have incarnated Jesus for me over the years:

Glen Kinnard	Harold Lile
Anne Kinnard	Mike Taliaferro
Chippy Brewer	Sam Powell
Leigh Kinnard	Barry Beaty
Aunt Dodda	Shane Engel
Neil Christy	Phil Garrison
Randall Burton	Matt Fridley
John R. Vaughn, Jr.	Phil Zayas
Dr. Porter King	The Macks
Bob Wheless	Chels and the D-Man

And many others who influenced my life.

You have your list. Be grateful for these people. They are the personal incarnation of Jesus to you.

Now ask yourself, to whom will you be the incarnation of Jesus? People are begging, "Give me some skin." They want to see Jesus. I believe it was Augustine who said, "The only Bible that most people will ever read is the one they see lived out in your life." I would add, "The first glimpse of Jesus that most people will ever see is the Jesus that they see lived out in your life." When people look at you, do they see a bit of Jesus living in you? Jesus took on our skin. Let's take on his skin and be the incarnation of Jesus for the entire world to see him living in us.

The Cross: Jesus Took on Our Sin

> Power, no matter how well-intentioned, tends to cause suffering. Love, being vulnerable, absorbs it. In a point of convergence on a hill called Calvary, God renounced the one for the sake of the other.[7]
>
> –Philip Yancey, Christian author

> Jesus, however, took upon himself all this suffering and lifted it up on the cross, not as a curse but as a blessing. Jesus

> made the cup of God's wrath into a cup of blessings. That's the mystery of the Eucharist. Jesus died for us so that we may live. He poured out his blood for us so that we may find new life. He gave himself away for us, so that we can live in community. He became for us food and drink so that we can be fed for everlasting life. That is what Jesus meant when he took the cup and said: "This cup is the new covenant in my blood poured out for you" (Luke 22:20).[8]
>
> –Henri J.M. Nouwen, spiritual writer and theologian

The place where we can most visibly see the heart of Jesus is in his Passion story. As Jesus is stretched vertically between heaven and earth on the cross, he is also stretched horizontally as his arms reach out to his right and to his left to embrace all of humanity in his death. He died for us all. He took our place on the cross, and in so doing; he showed us the depth of his love. He showed us his heart.

The Passion

Following is a series of verses from the Gospels, which I condensed and wove together to tell the passion story. As you read the story, place yourself in first-century Palestine and relive the events of Jesus' passion. Look for the heart of Jesus in the passion story. The story of the cross is the story of the heart of Jesus.

The Garden of Gethsemane

He took Peter and the two sons of Zebedee along with him, and he began to be sorrowful and troubled. Then he said to them, "My soul is overwhelmed with sorrow to the point of death. Stay here and keep watch with me."

Going a little father, he fell with his face to the ground and prayed, "My Father, if it is possible, may this cup be taken from me. Yet not as I will, but as you will" (Matthew 26:37-39).

An angel from heaven appeared to him and strengthened him. And being in anguish, he prayed more earnestly, and his sweat was like drops of blood falling to the ground (Luke 22:43-44).

The Arrest

With Judas was a large crowd armed with swords and clubs,

sent from the chief priests and the elders of the people.... Then the men stepped forward, seized Jesus and arrested him. With that, one of Jesus' companions reached for his sword, drew it out and struck the servant of the high priest, cutting off his ear.

"Put your sword back in its place," Jesus said to him, "for all who live by the sword will die by the sword. Do you think I cannot call on my Father, and he will at once put at my disposal more than twelve legions of angels?" (Matthew 26:47-55).

Jesus said, "But this is the hour when darkness reigns" (Luke 23:53).

Then the detachment of soldiers with its commander and the Jewish officials arrested Jesus. They bound him (John 18:12).

Then all the disciples deserted him and fled (Matt. 26:47-56).

The Sanhedrin/The High Priest

One of the officials nearby struck him (Jesus) in the face. "Is this the way you answer the high priest?" he demanded.

"If I said something wrong," Jesus replied, "Testify as to what is wrong. But if I spoke the truth, why did you strike me?" Then Annas sent him, still bound, to Caiaphas the high priest (John 18:22-24).

The high priest said to him, "I charge you under oath by the living God: Tell us if you are the Christ, the Son of God."

"Yes, it is as you say," Jesus replied. "But I say to all of you: in the future you will see the Son of Man sitting at the right hand of the Mighty One and coming on the clouds of heaven."

Then the high priest tore his clothes and said, "He has spoken blasphemy! Why do we need any more witnesses? Look, now you have heard the blasphemy. What do you think?"

"He is worthy of death," they answered.

Then they spit in his face and struck him with their fists. Others slapped him, and said, "Prophesy to us, Christ. Who hit you?" (Matthew 26:63-68).

The Guards

The men who were guarding Jesus began mocking and beating him. They blindfolded him and demanded, "Prophesy! Who hit you?" And they said many other insulting things to him (Luke 22: 63-64).

Before Pilate

Meanwhile Jesus stood before the governor, and the governor asked him, "Are you the king of the Jews?"

"Yes, it is as you say," Jesus replied (Matthew 27:11-12).

Before Herod

When Herod saw Jesus, he was greatly pleased…he hoped to see him perform some miracle. He plied him with many questions, but Jesus gave him no answer…Then Herod and his soldiers ridiculed and mocked him. Dressing him in an elegant robe, they sent him back to Pilate (Luke 23:8-11).

Back to Pilate

When Pilate saw that he was getting nowhere, but that instead an uproar was starting, he took water and washed his hands in front of the crowd. "I am innocent of this man's blood," he said. "It is your responsibility!"

All the people answered, "Let his blood be on us and on our children!"

Then he released Barabbas to them. But he had Jesus flogged (Matthew 27:24-26).

The Mock Coronation

Then the governor's soldiers took Jesus into the Praetorium and gathered the whole company of soldiers around him. They stripped him and put a scarlet robe on him, and then twisted together a crown of thorns and set it on his head. They put a staff in his right hand and knelt in front of him and mocked him. "Hail, king of the Jews!" they said. They spit on him, and took the staff and struck him on the head again and again. After they had mocked him, they took off the robe and put his own clothes on him (Matthew 27: 27-31).

Pilate's Judgment

Once more Pilate came out and said to the Jews, "Look, I am bringing him out to you to let you know that I find no basis for a charge against him." When Jesus came out wearing the crown of thorns and the purple robe, Pilate said to them, "Here is the man!"

As soon as the chief priests and their officials saw him, they shouted, "Crucify! Crucify!"...

"Where do you come from?" Pilate asked Jesus, but Jesus gave him no answer. "Do you refuse to speak to me?" Pilate said. "Don't you realize I have power either to free you or to crucify you?"

Jesus answered, "You would have no power over me if it were not given to you from above. Therefore the one who handed me over to you is guilty of a greater sin...."

Finally Pilate handed Jesus over to them to be crucified (John 19:9-16).

Simon of Cyrene

So the soldiers took charge of Jesus. Carrying his own cross, he went out to the place of the Skull (John 19:16-17).

A certain man from Cyrene, Simon, the father of Alexander and Rufus, was passing by on his way in from the country, and put the cross on him and made him carry it behind Jesus (Mark 15:21, Luke 22:26).

Golgotha

They came to a place called Golgotha (which means the Place of the Skull)....Where they crucified him... (Matthew 27:33-35).

The Crowd

Those who passed by hurled insults at him, shaking their heads and saying, "You who are going to destroy the temple and build it in three days, save yourself! Come down from the cross, if you are the Son of God!" (Matthew 27:39-40).

Jesus said, "Father, forgive them, for they do not know what they are doing" (Luke 23:34).

In the same way the chief priests, the teachers of the law and the elders mocked him. "He saved others," they said, "but he can't save himself! He's the King of Israel! Let him come down now from the cross, and we will believe in him. He trusts in God. Let God rescue him, for he said, 'I am the Son of God" (Matthew 27:41-43).

Jesus' Mother

Near the cross of Jesus stood his mother....When Jesus saw his mother there, and the disciple whom he loved standing nearby, he said to his mother, "Dear woman, here is your son," and to the disciple, "Here is your mother." From that time on this disciple took her into his home" (John 19:25-27).

The Death

From the sixth hour until the ninth hour darkness came over all the land (for the sun stopped shinning). About the ninth hour Jesus cried out in a loud voice, *"Eloi, Eloi, lama sabachthani?"*—which means, "My God, my God, why have you forsaken me?" (Matthew 27:45-50, Luke 23:45).

Later, knowing that all was now completed, and so that the Scripture would be fulfilled, Jesus said, "I am thirsty." A jar of wine vinegar was there, so they soaked a sponge in it, put the sponge on a stalk of the hyssop plant, and lifted it to Jesus' lips. When he had received the drink, (Jesus cried with a loud voice, he said, "It is finished: Father, into your hands I commit my spirit," and he bowed his head and gave up his spirit (John19:28-30, parenthesis includes part of Luke 23:46).

The Aftermath

At that moment the curtain of the temple was torn in two from top to bottom. The earth shook and the rocks split. The tombs broke open and the bodies of many holy people who had died were raised to life. They came out of the tombs, and after Jesus' resurrection they went into the holy city and appeared to many people.

When the centurion and those with him who were guarding Jesus saw the earthquake and all that had happened, they were terrified, and exclaimed, "Surely he was the Son of God!" (Matthew 27:51-54).

Nothing shows us the heart of Jesus like the passion and suffering of the cross. Nothing shows us the heart of the Father, Son, and Holy Spirit like the cross. The Father was willing to give up his Son on the cross. The Son was willing to bear the burden of our sin. And the Spirit was willing to struggle with Jesus on the cross.

After I watched Mel Gibson's *The Passion of the Christ*,[9] one character stood out to me. This was the portrayal of Simon of Cyrene. The evangelist Mark writes of Simon, "A certain man from Cyrene, Simon, the father of Alexander and Rufus, was passing by on his way from the country, and they forced him to carry the cross" (Mark 15:21).

Simon saw himself as an innocent bystander. He was from a small town in North Africa and was in Jerusalem to celebrate the Passover. He was dragged into the event of the cross by the Roman soldiers. When Jesus could carry the cross no longer, Simon was compelled by the Romans to carry it. The cross became Simon's cross. He thought he was an innocent bystander, but he wasn't. He was pulled into the passion story by forces that he could not control.

None of us are innocent bystanders in the story of the cross. We all deserve to carry the cross. The suffering of Jesus should be our suffering. Paul speaks to this in Romans 5:1-5:

> Therefore, since we have been justified through faith, we have peace with God through our Lord Jesus Christ, through whom we have gained access by faith into this grace in which we now stand. And we rejoice in the hope of the glory of God. Not only so, but we also rejoice in our sufferings, because we know that suffering produces perseverance, perseverance, character; and character, hope. And hope does not disappoint us, because God has poured out his love into our hearts by the Holy Spirit, whom he has given us.

In Mark's accounting of the event, he doesn't just mention Simon, but he also mentions his two sons, Alexander and Rufus? Why mention Alexander and Rufus? I believe it is because the community to whom Mark wrote knew Alexander and Rufus. How did they know them? I believe it is because they were disciples. How did they become disciples? They learned about Jesus through their father Simon. Simon became a follower of Jesus. After all, how could you carry the cross of Jesus and not become a disciple? Isn't carrying the cross of Jesus what being a disciple is all about?

The biggest controversy surrounding the movie, *The Passion of the Christ*, was concerning the matter of blame. Who should be blamed for the crucifixion of Jesus? Were the Jewish leaders to blame? How about Pilate, was he to blame? Were the Roman soldiers to blame? Was Judas, the betrayer, to blame? Was the bitter thief who was crucified next to Jesus to blame? How about the angry mob who shouted, "Crucify him!" Were these people guilty of the death of Jesus? The answer is "Yes." They were all guilty. But they weren't the only ones to blame. We are all to blame. All of humanity is guilty. It is our sin that put Jesus on the cross. The great Apostle Paul writes, "You see, at just the right time, when we were still powerless, Christ died for the ungodly. Very rarely will anyone die for a righteous man, though for a good man someone might possibly dare to die. But God demonstrates his own love for us in this: While we were still sinners, Christ died for us" (Romans 5:6-8).

Simon was not an innocent bystander. There were no innocent bystanders on that day. There are no innocent bystanders today. We all share in the blame of the cross. Therefore, we should all share the wounds of the cross. Consider this wonderful, meditative poem written by Amy Carmichael who served as a missionary to India:

No Scar?

Hast thou no scar?
No hidden scar on foot, or side, or hand?
I hear thee sung as mighty in the land,
I hear them hail thy bright ascendant star,
Hast thou no scar?
Hast thou no wound?
Yet I was wounded by the archers, spent,
Leaned Me against a tree to die; and rent
By ravening beasts that encompassed Me, I swooned:
Hast thou no wound?
No wound? No scar?
Yet, as the Master shall the servant be,
And pierced are the feet that follow Me;
But thine are whole: can he have followed far
Who has no wound nor scar?[10]

The Body: The Skin We Are In

Earlier, I commented that we, the church, need to be the incarnation of Jesus for people today. In the same way that he took on our skin, we need to take on his skin. When we take on his skin, we need to realize that his skin is scarred and wounded by the crucifixion. We don't just take on the skin of Jesus. We also take on his scars. This will help us remember that his death on the cross was for our sins. His scars are our scars. His wounds are our wounds. And by his wounds, we are healed.

Dear Abba,

Thank you for sending your Son, Jesus, to take on our skin so that we might see more clearly how much you empathize with our sufferings, our hurts, our weaknesses, our longings, our failings, our wounds, our struggles and our pain.

Thank you, because while Jesus was still in our skin he was also willing to take on our sin and die on the cross for us. Help us to understand that we are not just innocent bystanders at the cross—we are to blame. And help us, just as Jesus took on our skin and our sin, to take on his scars in discipleship to him.

In the name of Jesus
Amen

Footnotes

[1] C.S. Lewis, *Mere Christianity* (New York: Macmillan, 1956), 148-149.

[2] Willard, *The Divine Conspiracy*, 94-95.

[3] The words in brackets are mine.

[4] Manning, *Restless Heart* (San Francisco: Harper San Francisco, 2000), 90-91.

[5] Eugene H. Peterson, *The Message* (Colorado Springs: NavPress, 2002), 1916.

[6] Scazzero, 175.

[7] Philip Yancey, *The Jesus I Never Knew* (Grand Rapids: Zondervan Publishing House, 1995), 205.

[8] Henri J.M. Nouwen, *Can You Drink the Cup?* (Notre Dame: Ave Maria Press, 1996), 68.

[9] *The Passion of the Christ*, Directed by Mel Gibson, Produced by Mel Gibson, Bruce Davey, Stephen McEveety, Icon Productions, 2004.

[10] Found in Terry Wardle's *The Transforming Path* (Siloam Springs, Arkansas: Leafwood Publishers, 2003), 143.

Chapter Eight

The Heart of the Spirit

> The Spirit begins the process of growth by wooing us to Jesus, and he is working to finish the task.[1]
>
> –Cloud and Townsend, Christian psychologists

> The Spirit indwells in human history to attest God the Father and God the Son; to draw together the called-out people for celebration and proclamation; to reveal the truth to those yielded to the Spirit's promptings; to equip for service; to seal the promise of things to come; to elicit faith, hope, and love; and to redress the history of sin.[2]
>
> –Thomas C. Oden, professor of theology

Do You Know the Spirit?

The great Apostle Paul asked his audience in ancient Ephesus, "Did you receive the Holy Spirit when you believed?" They answered, "No, we have not even heard that there is a Holy Spirit" (Acts19:2). I have often thought that if Paul were to come to our churches, he might have the very same question for us, "Did you receive the Holy Spirit when you believed?" We don't often speak about the Spirit. He is the least discussed of the Trinity. He doesn't get equal time. Why is that?

I know that I have had a less than perfect understanding of the Spirit. I've been afraid to talk about the Spirit. I would say, "God led me to this decision." I would say, "Jesus answered my prayer." But I would never say, "The Spirit showed me the way." Perhaps you can relate. Why is this? I think there are several reasons why. Consider the following:

- When I was growing up, the Holy Spirit was known as the Holy Ghost. In older translations like the King James Version, the term "Holy Ghost" was used instead of Holy Spirit. And I didn't want to have anything to do with ghosts. This term,

"Holy Ghost," gave the Spirit a mystical, ethereal, otherworldly quality. The term stripped him of personhood. He didn't have the personal quality that the Father and Son possessed. He became less relatable; therefore, he wasn't discussed as much as the Father or the Son.

- My teenage years coincided with the rise of the Charismatic/Pentecostal movement. I heard many strange stories about the Holy Ghost. One story was that a child, daughter of a famous entertainer, prayed for the Holy Ghost to raise her pet hamster from the dead, and that the Holy Ghost answered her prayer and brought her pet back from the dead. Strange things like this seemed to be part and parcel of the charismatic movement. I thought it best to stay away from such things; therefore, best to stay away from talking about the Holy Spirit.
- I couldn't understand the person, the nature or the role of the Holy Spirit. What we don't understand, we fear. Therefore, I was afraid to talk about the Holy Spirit.
- Some members of the church spoke of the Holy Spirit as being an "it" and not a "he." Many still do. This takes away the personhood of the Holy Spirit. This caused me to think of the Holy Spirit as a thing and not as a person. The Bible describes him as comforting, teaching, guiding, instructing, calling and sending. These are all personal attributes. Until we see that the Holy Spirit has personhood and personality, we will have a difficult time relating to him.
- I viewed Charismatics and Pentecostals as driven by emotion, and I believed that religion should be driven by the intellect. I didn't want to drift into Pentecostalism. Now I realize that I turned my back on the Holy Spirit because I did not share certain beliefs about what his power could do. This was a grave error. We need the power of the Holy Spirit in our ministries.
- When I was growing up, many conservative Biblical scholars taught that the Holy Spirit did not perform any task outside what the Bible could do for us. Since the Spirit guided the early church to all truth, some equated the Spirit with the Word of God—the Bible. They taught that the Spirit did not operate outside the Word of God. This idea limits our conversation about the Holy Spirit.

All of this led me to conclude that the Holy Ghost/Holy Spirit was too scary, too misunderstood, too emotional or too controversial for me to get my arms around. I could easily relate to the Father and the Son, but I couldn't begin to understand the person, nature or work of the Spirit. So the Spirit became the missing part of the Trinity.

That being said, I want to also say that I was a closet fan of the Holy Spirit. I would watch television programs where people would get slain in the Spirit, and I would be envious of their experience. I wanted some of what they had. My religion had no emotion to it. I could connect with God only on an intellectual level. Our church services were staid and quiet. No one even dared to say "Amen." Our teen devotionals were serious and joyless. Very little humor was used. I wanted to experience God in a different way. I wanted to know what "holy laughter" was. I wanted to "sing, shout and dance all about" in church. There had to be a way to experience God on a more emotional level.

The Church of Christ has generally defined the Holy Spirit by what he is not or what he does not do. This is never a good way to define someone. Imagine defining Jesus only by stating what he is not. But that is exactly what we have done with the Spirit. We have said:

- The Holy Spirit is not passed on through the laying on of hands.
- The miraculous gifts of the Holy Spirit are not operative today.
- You cannot be baptized in the Holy Spirit today.
- The Holy Spirit does not operate outside the Word of God.
- It is not possible to blaspheme the Holy Spirit today.

I have heard the Holy Spirit defined in all these ways. This way of thinking about the Holy Spirit is very negative and limiting. I want to view God's Holy Spirit in a more positive and experiential way. Don't tell me what the Holy Spirit can't do today. Tell me what he can do. Thomas C. Oden, professor of theology at Drew University speaks positively of the work of the Holy Spirit when he writes:

> The work of the one Spirit is indicated by varied names ascribed in scripture. As compassionate Lord, the Spirit is Comforter (John 14:16); as reclaimer, the Spirit of adoption (Romans 8:

> 15); as regenerator, the Spirit of Life (Romans 8:2); as the life giver, the Spirit who awakens faith (2 Corinthians 4:13); as merciful One, the Spirit of Grace (Hebrews 10:29); as teacher, the Spirit of Truth (John 14:17); as counselor, the Spirit of Wisdom (Ephesians 1:17); as sanctifier, the Spirit of holiness (Romans 1:14).[3]

This tells me something positive about the Holy Spirit. This is what I want to know about him.

Who is the Holy Spirit? How can he work in my life today? What is the gift of the Holy Spirit that I received at baptism? What is the heart of the Holy Spirit? These are matters that I would like for us to discuss openly as brothers and sisters.

Who is this Spirit that indwells us?[4]

- He is powerful. He was the moving force in creation.
- He is truthful. He is called, "The Spirit of Truth."
- He has a giving heart. He gives life, gives strength, gives comfort and gives aid.
- He intercedes with the Father on our behalf (Romans 8:26).
- He is our constant companion (Psalm 139:7).
- He moves the church forward (Acts 20:28).
- He is an invisible wind (John 3:8).
- He is an active change agent in our lives (Psalm 7:9, Proverbs 20:27, Romans 8:27, 1 Corinthians 2:10).
- He is a cleansing water (John 7:37-38).
- He is a purging fire (Exodus 13:21).
- He will lead and guide us (Psalm 143:10; John 16:13; Acts 13: 4).
- He is an innocent dove (Matthew 3:16).
- He is our counselor/our advocate (John 14:26).
- He is our *paraklatos.*
- He is our *ruach.*
- He is the *hagios pneumata.*

Let me say it again—the Holy Spirit is the most misunderstood member of the Trinity. He is often the forgotten member of the Trinity. It is time we began talking about the Holy Spirit with the same respect that we use when we speak of God the Father or God the Son. The Holy Spirit is God. He has personhood and personality. He indwells our lives. He has heart. We need to understand his heart. As we understand the heart of the Holy Spirit, we will better understand what it means to be spiritual beings.

I'm afraid we might be treating the Holy Spirit the way most New Yorkers treat the New York Mets baseball team—with little or no respect. I heard a joke recently about how the coach of the New York Mets and the coach of the New York Yankees were traveling to a news conference together when they had an accident and both died. They woke up in heaven, and after getting registered there, they took a tour of the place. The tour guide wanted to show them their homes. He took the Mets' coach to his home first. It was a nice two-story brick home with all types of orange and blue Mets flags and pennants hanging from the windows. They went inside to look around. While they were looking upstairs, the Mets coach looked outside his window and saw an enormous white mansion on the hill above him decked out with blue and white flags and pennants of the New York Yankees. The Mets coach asked the tour guide, "My house is nice, but why does the coach of the Yankees get that gigantic mansion on the top of the hill?" The tour guide answered, "Oh, you're mistaken. That's not the coach's house. That's God's house."

Having lived around New York City for the past twenty years, I have come to see how little respect the Mets get. The Yankees rule New York. I wonder if we haven't treated the Holy Spirit a bit like the Mets get treated in New York. We often think about God the Father. We spend most of our time teaching and reading about God the Son. But we spend relatively little time thinking, talking or reading about God the Holy Spirit. When is the last time you sat in a class and had an open, frank, honest discussion about the Holy Spirit? He is the least discussed and the least understood of the Trinity. Professor Oden writes, "The modern tendency is to depersonalize the Spirit, to treat God the Spirit as reducible to an idea of spirituality or an attribute of God, rather than God's own personal meeting with persons living in history. This has contributed to the neglect and misunderstanding of the subject."[5] Since this is the case, we often miss out on the power that is available through the Holy Spirit. Although we cannot give an exhaustive study of the Holy Spirit here, we can take a look at the heart of the Holy Spirit. By looking at his heart, we can open our hearts to allow God's Holy Spirit to work in our lives.

The Characteristics of the Holy Spirit

If someone were to ask you who the Holy Spirit is, how would you answer him or her? Do you know enough about the person, nature and work of the Holy Spirit to speak intelligently about him? The Bible has much to say about the Holy Spirit. The Bible lists many characteristics of the Spirit. These characteristics speak to the personhood, personality, person, nature, work, function, purpose and role of the Holy Spirit.

Guiding (Romans 8:14)
Life-giving (John 6:63)
Convicting (John 16:8)
Interceding (Romans 8:26)
Comforting (John 14:18)
Calling (Acts 13:2)
Commissioning (Acts 20:28)
Bearing witness to our spirit that we are children of God (Romans 8:16)
Revealing what is yet to come (John 16:13)
He searches our hearts (1 Corinthians 2:20-11)
We can resist the Spirit (Acts 7:51)
We can answer the Spirit (Acts 10:19-21)
We can vex the Spirit (Isaiah 63:10)
We can grieve the Spirit (Ephesians 4:30)
We can quench the Spirit (1 Thessalonians 5:19)
We can blaspheme the Spirit (Matthew 12:31-32, Mark 3:27-28, Luke 10:12)
We can lie to the Spirit (Acts 5:3-9)

What Does The Holy Spirit Do For Us?

The Spirit is our Helper: John 14:15-27

The Holy Spirit is our *paraklatos*. This word can be translated as "counselor, advocate, helper or aid." In the King James Bible it was translated as "comforter." But at that time in history to comfort someone meant, "to give them strength." The verb, *parakaleo*, means "to call alongside, to exhort, to aid, to encourage, to strengthen, to help." This is what the Holy Spirit does. This is also who he is. This is his heart. He wants to encourage us. He wants to strengthen us. He is our helper. He is there to lift us up when we fall. And we are going to fall. He picks us up when we are down. And we are going to feel down. He claps for us when we do great things for God. And we are going to do great things for God. He is our personal, spiritual trainer. He is our motivational coach. He is the encouraging friend who always has something positive to say.

But we ask, "If the Holy Spirit is all these things, then why don't I feel him in my life?" "Why don't I feel his encouragement?" "Why does he not strengthen me?" Perhaps we are out of step with the Spirit. Paul writes, "Since we live by the Spirit, let us keep in step with the Spirit" (Galatians 5:25). To keep in step with the Spirit, we must think about the Spirit. We must strive to let God's Spirit live in our lives and take over our minds. We must become full of the Holy Spirit.

The Apostle Paul had much to say on this point in Romans 8. Consider his words:

> And so Jesus condemned sin in sinful man, in order that the righteous requirements of the law might be fully met in us, who do not live according to the sinful nature but according to the Spirit. Those who live according to the sinful nature have their minds set on what that nature desires; but those who live in accordance with the Spirit have their minds set on what the Spirit desires. The mind of the sinful man is death, but the mind controlled by the Spirit is life and peace; the sinful mind is hostile to God. It does not submit to God's law, nor can it do so. Those controlled by the sinful nature cannot please God.
>
> The Spirit, however, controls you, not by the sinful nature but, if the Spirit of God lives in you. And if anyone does not have the Spirit of Christ, he does not belong to Christ. But if Christ is in you, your body is dead because of sin, yet your spirit is alive because of righteousness. And if the Spirit of him who raised Jesus from the dead is living in you, he who raised Christ from the dead will also give life to your mortal bodies through his Spirit who lives in you.

Paul has many positive things to say about the Holy Spirit. I especially want to focus in on what he says in verse five, "Those who live according to the sinful nature have their minds set on what that nature desires; but those who live in accordance with the Spirit have their minds set on what the Spirit desires." In the Greek this is even more concise, "those who think according to the flesh are of the flesh; those according to the Spirit are of the Spirit." Let that sink in. "Those according to the Spirit are of the Spirit." Or even more concise, "According to the Spirit/Of the Spirit." Or even more concise, "Think Spirit/Get Spirit."

If we are going to live according to the Spirit, then we have to focus on the Spirit. We can resist the Spirit, vex the Spirit, quench the Spirit and grieve the Spirit. We can also focus on the Spirit and let him live in our lives.

We have to retrain our focus. Around 1850, a German researcher named Hermann Helmholtz discovered something very interesting. Morton Hunt in *The Story of Psychology* relates the following story:

> It occurred to him (Hermann Helmholtz) that if he could distort the spatial sensations reaching a subject's brain—and if his theory was correct—the subject should adapt to the distorted vision and learn to interpret it correctly. He therefore constructed eyeglasses with prismatic lenses that shifted the apparent position of objects to the right of where they actually were. When subjects wearing the glasses tried to touch objects in front of them, they missed—they reached toward the apparent rather than the real position of the objects.
>
> Next, for some minutes he had them reach for and handle the objects while wearing the lenses; at first they had to consciously reach to the left of where they saw the object, but soon they began to reach for objects where they actually were without having to think about it. They had make a perceptual adaptation; their minds had reinterpreted the messages arriving from the optic nerves and they now saw the objects in the context of reality.
>
> Finally, when they took off the spectacles and reached for the objects, they missed again, this time erring to the left of the real position; it took a little while for their normal space orientation to reassert itself.[6]

When it comes to the Holy Spirit, our perception is off. We need to retrain our thinking. We aren't focused on the Spirit; therefore, we miss him. Remember: According to the Spirit/Of the Spirit. Remember: Think Spirit/Get Spirit.

Some might ask: "What about when I sin?" They wonder: "What happens to the Holy Spirit when I sin?" According to John 16:7-11 the Holy Spirit doesn't stop working on us when we sin, but he begins to work overtime to convict us of sin. That is his heart. He wants to convict the world that sin is wrong. Jesus says:

> But I tell you the truth: It is for your good that I am going away. Unless I go away, the Counselor will not come to you; but if I go, I will send him to you. When he comes, he will convict the world of guilt in regard to sin and righteousness and judgment: in regard to sin, because men do not believe in me; in regard to righteousness, because I am going to the Father, where you can see me no longer; and in regard to judgment, because the prince of this world now stands condemned.

I don't know if you ever saw the movie *Moonstruck* or not. It is a romantic comedy set in an Italian neighborhood in Brooklyn starring Cher and Nicolas Cage. Cher won an Academy Award for her performance in the movie. When my wife and I first saw the movie, we were living in an Italian neighborhood in Brooklyn. The movie was like looking outside our apartment window. In the movie, Nicolas Cage's character is a young, one-armed baker who falls in love with an older Italian woman in the neighborhood. The woman is played by Cher. Cage's character is "moonstruck" by Cher's character. In order to bring Cage to his senses and get him to see that his affection is misplaced, Cher slaps him in face with a powerful blow from the palm of her hand and says, "Snap out of it!" It is the greatest scene in the movie. "Snap out of it!"

I can't believe I'm using a movie with Cher in it to illustrate the Holy Spirit, but that is exactly what I'm doing. When we give our lives over to sin, the Holy Spirit begins to work overtime to convict us of sin and he says, "Snap out of it!" He doesn't leave us. He doesn't abandon us. We often feel he does, but this is just wrong. In fact, he works all the more to convict us of the wrongness of our actions and to get us to repent. He is there working alongside us to create change. He will exhort us, rebuke us or discipline us if he has to. But he wants us to see that sin is wrong. He says to us, "Snap out it!"

The Holy Spirit is Our Guide: Romans 8:12-17, John 16:13

Are we led by God's Spirit? We need a guide. This is a perilous journey that we have undertaken. The journey of the heart is filled with slippery slopes and dangerous pitfalls. It is not the broad, easy way of legalism. We need help navigating the way of the heart. We need a guide. Much is written in today's religious writings about spiritual mentors and spiritual guides. Spiritual guides are helpful on our journey. But why go to a mere person for spiritual guidance, when the Holy Spirit wants to be your guide? Learn to allow the Spirit to guide you on your journey.

John Eldredge has written an excellent book that really resonates with me entitled, *Waking the Dead*. In this book he talks about our need for spiritual guidance on our journey in life. He writes:

> If you're not pursuing a dangerous quest with your life, well, then, you don't need a Guide. If you haven't found yourself in the midst of a ferocious war, then you won't need a seasoned Captain. If you've settled in your mind to live as though this is a fairly neutral world and you are simply trying to live your life as best you can, then you can probably get by with the Christianity of tips and techniques. Maybe. I'll give you about a fifty-fifty chance. But if you intend to live in the story that God is telling, and if you want the life he offers, then you are going to need more than a handful of principles, however noble they may be. There are too many twists and turns in the road ahead, too many ambushes waiting only God know where, too much at stake. You cannot possibly prepare yourself for every situation. Narrow is the way, said Jesus. How shall we be sure to find it? We need God intimately, and we need him desperately.
>
> "You have made known to me the path of life," David said (Ps. 16:11). Yes—that's it. In all the ins and outs of this thing we call living, there is one narrow path to life, and we need help finding it.[7]

In J. R. R. Tolkien's masterpiece *The Two Towers*[8] (If you've only seen the movies and not read the trilogy, then you haven't fully experienced Middle Earth) Frodo Baggins and Sam Gamgee turn toward Mordor in hope of destroying the evil ring of power. Many problems lie ahead for them. But as they begin the journey they have one major problem—they don't know the way. They need a guide. Unfortunately, for them, the only guide is an untrustworthy character named Gollum. Gollum has been to the dark tower. He knows the way. Frodo and Sam must trust Gollum. Without a guide, even an untrustworthy guide, they have no hope of destroying the ring. So Gollum becomes their guide.

We need a guide. We have a perilous journey ahead of us. We must journey through the swamps of pride, lust, hatred, even self-hatred, folly and worldliness. Unlike the aforementioned hobbits, we have a trustworthy guide—the Holy Spirit. We can trust his guidance. But how does he guide us?

He guides us:

- Through the Word
- Through people
- Through experience
- And for lack of better expression—through guidance

Yes, the Holy Spirit guides us through guidance. John Eldredge writes, "Walking with God is a way of life. It's something to be learned; our ability to hear God's voice and discern his word grows over time, as Brother Lawrence said it, 'We practice the presence of God.'"[9] "Hearing God's voice," "discerning his word," "practicing his presence" all these grand ideas fall under the guidance of the Holy Spirit.

Why can't the Holy Spirit make us aware of his choices in the here and now? We talk about an "epiphany," a "stroke of genius," a "moment of clarity." Why do we not speak of a "Holy Spirit moment?"

In Joel 2 and Acts 2 God promised that he would reveal his intentions to men through dreams and visions. It happened once, why not now? Maybe if we opened our lives to the guidance of the Holy Spirit, then he would guide us.

This I know:
If I'm not looking for the Spirit's guidance,
If I'm not listening for his voice,
If I'm not asking the Spirit to lead me,
Then I'll never see him when he does appear.

If my mind is closed,
If I don't believe that the Spirit will guide me,
Then he will have no opportunity to work in my life.

If I can't imagine him coming to me,
If I can't picture him strengthening me,
If I can't perceive of him guiding me,
Then even if he were to guide me,
I wouldn't know that he was there.

I need to open my mind to the Holy Spirit working in my life.

Are we open to the Spirit of God working in a special way in our lives? Dallas Willard, my favorite contemporary theologian, writes:

> The doleful reality is that very few human beings really do concretely desire to hear what God has to say to them. This is shown by how rarely we listen for his voice when we are not in trouble or when we are not being faced with a decision that we do not know how to handle. People who understand and warmly desire to hear God's voice will, by contrast, want to hear it when life is uneventful just as much as they want to hear it when they are facing trouble or big decisions. This is a test that we should all apply to ourselves as we go in search of God's word: do we seek it only under uncomfortable circumstances? Our answer may reveal that our failure to hear his voice when we want to is due to the fact that we do not in general want to hear it, that we want it only when we think we need it.[10]

I very much agree with Dr. Willard on this point. I believe that we are very inept at listening for God's voice. I also believe that ineptitude comes from a lack of desire.

What do I mean when I talk about being guided by the Holy Spirit? I'm not talking about being like Joan of Arc or Joan of Arcadia. I am a disciple who wants the Holy Spirit to guide me in my everyday life. And if seeking his guidance means only that it draws me closer to the Spirit and makes me a more spiritual and spirit-filled person, then that is enough. But I want to be open for a fuller experience of the Spirit. I want to make sure that the door is open for the Spirit to work in my life. For most of my life the door has been closed. I wouldn't have recognized the Spirit even if he had busted through the door, thrown me on the floor, slapped me in the face and announced what he was doing. At the very least, I need to leave the door open for him to work in my life.

Remember: According to the Spirit/Of the Spirit. Remember: Think Spirit/Get Spirit.

Until recently, if anyone had asked me if I believed that the Holy Spirit spoke to me, first, I would have given them the harshest look that I could have mustered, then, I would have answered them with a categorical and unequivocal, "No!" But that was until recently. In recent days, I have opened my mind to listening to the promptings of the Holy Spirit. In doing so, I now understand that the Holy Spirit is able to speak to my heart. And why not? The Spirit spoke to God's men throughout the Bible, why would he not wish to communicate with me today? Dallas Willard writes, "There is nothing in Scripture to indicate that the biblical modes of God's communication with humans have been superseded or abolished by either the presence of the church or the close of the scriptural canon."[11] I believe that Dr. Willard is correct. Just because the Word of God is a complete canon that does not mean that the Holy Spirit cannot communicate the will of God to me on a particular matter. If God does not speak to us outside his word, is this not the same as biblical deism? How is this different than the Sadducees of Jesus' day?

I'm not talking about speaking in tongues. I'm not talking about being slain in the Spirit. I'm not talking about holy barking or holy laughter. I'm not talking about getting all Pentecostal on Sundays. I'm just saying—let's make sure we are open to the Spirit's promptings Let's make sure we are open to the Spirit moving and working in our lives.

We must open our eyes and expect miracles. We must trust that God's Spirit will lead, and we must listen for his voice. We must allow God's Spirit to rejuvenate our lives. Instead of an epiphany or a moment of clarity or a stroke of genius, we should think in terms of a "Spirit moment." And when we have that moment, lets give the Spirit his props.

The heart of the Spirit is a helping heart. The heart of the Spirit is a heart that offers us guidance. We must open our heart to receive the heart of the Spirit in our lives. Remember: According to the Spirit/Of the Spirit. Remember: Think Spirit/Get Spirit.

The Prayer of An Unknown Confederate Soldier

I asked God for strength that I might achieve,
I was made weak that I might learn humbly to obey.
I asked for health that I might do better things.
I was given infirmity that I might do better things.
I asked for riches that I might be happy;
I was given poverty that I might be wise.
I asked for power when I was young that I might have the praise of men;
I was given weakness that I might feel the need for God.
I asked for all things that I might enjoy life;
I was given life that I might enjoy all things.
I got nothing that I asked for,
But everything I had hoped for.
Almost despite myself, my unspoken prayers were answered.
I am, among all people, most richly blessed.[12]

O God, send your Holy Spirit. Let your Spirit become mine, and let my own mind and spirit be forever brought to nothing! I give myself over to that Spirit of love and truth. Let him illumine me today and teach me to be gentle and lowly in heart.[13]

–François Fenelon,
17th century French devotional writer

Endnotes

[1] Cloud and Townsend, 96.

[2] Thomas C. Oden, *Life In the Spirit. Systematic Theology: Volume Three* (San Francisco: Harper San Francisco, 1992), 14.

[3] Ibid, 16.

[4] Compiled from material in Oden's *Life in the Spirit*, 16-ff.

[5] Ibid, 20.

[6] Morton Hunt, *The Story of Psychology* (New York: Anchor Press, 1994), 120-121.

[7] Eldredge, *Waking the Dead*, 95.

[8] J.R.R. Tolkien, *The Two Towers,* Second Edition (Boston: Houghton Mifflin Company), 1965.

[9] Ibid, 103.

[10] Willard, *Hearing God: Developing A Conversational Relationship With God* (Downers Grove: Intervarsity, 1984), 197.

[11] Ibid, 103.

[12] This widely disseminated text is alleged to have been taken from the pocket of a Confederate soldier who died in battle during the American Civil War. The original source is unknown.

[13] Fenelon, 137-138.

Part Four

The Heart of the Commandments

Here's how we can be sure that we know God in the right way: Keep his commandments.

If someone claims, "I know him well!" but doesn't keep his commandments, he's obviously a liar. His life doesn't match his words. But the one who keeps God's word is the person in whom we see God's mature love. This is the only way to be sure we're in God. Anyone who claims to be intimate with God ought to live the same kind of life Jesus lived.[1]

–1 John 2:3-5 in Eugene H. Peterson's *The Message*

Chapter Nine

The Greatest Command

When we tell God we love him with all our heart, often we are just using words, making a speech that has no reality. From our childhood on, many of us have been taught to speak in such a way, and so we continue to do so when we have grown up—often without knowing what we are saying.

But to love God means to have no will other than his. It means to faithfully observe his holy law. It means to have a horror of sin. To love God means to love what Jesus loved—poverty, humiliation, suffering. It means to hate what Jesus hated—the world, our pride, our passions.[2]

–François Fenelon, 17th century French devotional writer

There are times when it is good to step back and look at some of the fundamental precepts of Christianity and see how we are doing in these areas. There is a time to get back to basics.

One great way to get back to basics is to restudy the teachings of Jesus. He was the Master Teacher who taught us how to have a relationship with God.

The way of the heart must be based upon the teachings of Jesus. What did Jesus have to say about having a relationship with the Father? What did he teach about following the law versus having a heart for God? If Jesus were asked to pinpoint the most important aspect of having a relationship with God, what would his answer be? Let's see what Jesus has to say about the way of the heart.

The Greatest Commandment

Matthew 22:34-40, Mark 12:28-31, Luke 10:25-28

The context of this passage in Mark and Matthew is the same. Many of the religious leaders who excel at following the way of legalism came to Jesus to test him and to question him about the law. The Pharisees tested him by asking a question about taxes. The Sadducees followed up by asking a question concerning the resurrection. Then a scribe (a lawyer or theologian) asked Jesus a question, "What is the greatest commandment?" This was a question that was commonly debated in Judaism. One answer that was often given to this question was to quote the *Shema Israel* as found in Deuteronomy 6:4, "Hear, Oh Israel, the Lord your God is one." This was a great propositional truth. It was a truth accepted by the Jewish people. It was a distinguishing mark of Judaism. But propositional truth does not teach relationship. Jesus wanted to go beyond propositional truth to talk about relationship. Therefore, Jesus added, "Love the Lord your God with all your heart, soul, mind and strength."

Jesus makes sure that we place great value on relationship and not just on propositional truth. Truth is important. But truth without relationship quickly evolves into legalism. M. Robert Mulholland, Jr. in his wonderful book *Invitation to Journey*, writes:

> The Christian's identity and value do not reside in the fragile order and tenuous control that she or he imposes upon life. Identity and value are found in a vital and living relationship with Christ as Lord. This relationship liberates Christians from dependence upon their little systems of order and fragile structures of control. Not that believers live without order or control, but they are liberated from dependency on those systems and structures for their sense of self.[3]

Jesus teaches that the greatest command is to love God. Love is *agape* love. It is an unconditional, committed love. It is love that knows no boundaries. It is a love that is a consuming fire. It is a love that overwhelms us. It is emotional, romantic and intellectual.

Jesus teaches that our love for God must include our whole being. We must love him with all that makes us a person. We must withhold nothing from him. This love takes the whole of our heart (*kardia*). In the first century, the heart was looked upon as the seat of the emotions. It includes our passion. Our love for God must include our soul (*psuche*). The soul is what makes us an individual person. It is our personality, our personhood; it is who we are as a person. We must give God the whole of our mind (*dianoia*); God wants us to give him our intellect. He wants us to comprehend him on an intellectual level. He also wants the whole of our strength (*ischuos*). Our strength is our drive, our will, our desires and our actions. All of these attributes make us who we are as a people. God wants all of us. To give him our intellect without our emotions isn't enough. To give him our emotions, but to hold back our drive and will isn't pleasing either. He wants everything that we are.

R. T. France, in his commentary on Matthew writes, "Heart, soul and mind are not different 'parts' of man, but different ways of thinking of the whole man in relation to God."[4] D.A. Carson echoes this sentiment in his two-volume commentary, "From the viewpoint of biblical anthropology, "heart," "soul," and "mind" are not mutually exclusive but overlapping categories, together demanding our love for God to come from our whole person, our every faculty and capacity."[5]

Is your whole person, every faculty and capacity of you, in love with God? Is this love a fully committed, unconditional love of God? This is the greatest commandment. We must be consumed by our love for God. This is basic and fundamental to Christianity.

Do we **LOVE** God?

The greatest question is not, "Do we love God?" The greatest question is, "Do we **LOVE** God?" We must **LOVE** God with an *agape* **LOVE**. He must consume us. We must **LOVE** God with every faculty of our being, with all the capacity of our **LOVE**. Do we **LOVE** God?

Do you know what it is like to be consumed by love? Have you ever been so in love that it hurts? Have you ever been head over heals, crazy, punch-drunk, silly, stupid, madly in love with someone?

The first time I ever felt this way about someone was in college when I met Chippy Leigh Brewer. She was the prettiest girl I had ever seen. She had big, beautiful, hazel eyes; curly brown hair, a great smile, the craziest laugh that you ever heard in your life, and more personality that any one person was allowed to have. When we started dating, I was consumed by love for her. In class—I would think of her. I got up for breakfast, just to see her. I would say goodnight to her at her dormitory, walk back to my room and call her on the phone. It's a good thing that cell phone didn't exist back in the late '70s or I would still be paying for those cell phone bills.

I was consumed by love for her. G.K. Chesterton wrote, "Romance is the deepest thing in life, romance is deeper even than reality."[6] The romantic love that I felt in college for the girl who would become my wife was the deepest emotion that I had ever experienced in life up to that point. It would only get deeper the more I fell in love with her. But I had never felt that type of love for God. I never thought of being in love with God that deeply. I never allowed myself to think about being romantically in love with God. I always thought of loving God in an intellectual way. But perhaps the truest connection that we can make with God is in a romantic way. This is what it means to be consumed by our love for God. Are you head over heels, crazy, nuts, silly about him? Are you so in love that your love doesn't have an off switch? Do you think of him all the time? Do you long for him? This is being in **LOVE** with God. We should have desire, heart, passion. It should be magical, mystical, spiritual, unquantifiable, huge, ferocious, gigantic **LOVE**. It should be **LOVE** that is beyond us, special and extra-ordinary. Is this the kind of **LOVE** we have for God?

Oswald Chambers calls this type of love a "haunting." In his devotional classic, *My Utmost For His Highest*, he writes:

> What are you haunted by? You will say—By nothing, but we are all haunted by something, generally by ourselves, or, if we are Christians, by our experience. The Psalmist says we are to be haunted by God. The abiding consciousness of the life is to be with God, not thinking about Him. The whole of our life inside and out is to be absolutely haunted by the presence of God. A child's consciousness is so mother-haunted that although the child is not consciously thinking of its mother, yet when calamity arises, the relationship that abides is that of the mother. So we are to live and move and have our being in God, to look at everything in relation to God, because the abiding consciousness of God pushes itself to the front all the time.
>
> If we are haunted by God, nothing else can get in, no cares, no tribulation, no anxieties. We see now why Our Lord so emphasized the sin of worry. How can we dare be so utterly unbelieving when God is round about us? To be haunted by God is to have an effective barricade against all the onslaughts of the enemy.[7]

Agape **LOVE** is a haunting **LOVE**. This is the type of love that we must have for God. To have this type of love for God is to follow the way of the heart.

Trading True Love for a Cheap Imitation

Some of us might have had a consuming love for God before, but traded it in for a cheap imitation—a legalistic love. This is where you trade being in love with God for doing things for God. You change desire—I want to **LOVE** God—for ought—I ought to do this for God. This was the mistake of the Pharisees in Jesus' day (Matthew 23).

One way of doing this is to create a checklist of things that we ought to do instead of focusing on our desire to be close to God.

This checklist might include:

- Reading my Bible for 20 minutes each day.
- Praying for 15 minutes every day.
- Meeting at least one new person every week.
- Getting with a prayer partner every week.
- Encouraging a weak brother or sister every day.
- Serving someone this week.

Obviously there is nothing wrong with any item on this list. In fact these items should be the natural outpouring of our love for God. But we often trade a head-over-heels, consuming **LOVE** for God with a checklist of duty, service, doing and acting.

This checklist makes life easier in the short term because we can check off what we think is expected of us. We do our duty; we fulfill legalistic righteousness; we feel good about checking items off the list.

But in the long run, when we fail to meet the requirements of the list, we feel guilty. We begin to equate the checklist with our love for God. We honor God with our checklist, but our hearts are far from him.

Loving God should be about desire, heart and a consuming **LOVE**. Brent Curtis and John Eldredge speak of the difference between have an checklist love for God and a consuming **LOVE** for God in their wonderful book, *The Sacred Romance.* They write:

> The religious technocrats of Jesus' day confronted him with what they believed were the standards of a life pleasing to God. The external life, they argued, the life of ought and duty and service, was what mattered. "You're dead wrong," Jesus said. "In fact, you're just plain dead [whitewashed tombs]. What God cares about is the inner life, the life of the heart" (Matt.

> 23:25-28). Throughout the Old and New Testaments, the life of the heart is clearly God's central concern. When the people of Israel fell into totally external life of ritual and observance, God lamented, "These people...honor me with their lips, but their hearts are far from me" (Isaiah 29:13).
>
> Our heart is the key to the Christian life.
>
> The apostle Paul informs us that hardness of heart is behind all the addictions and evils of the human race (Romans 1:21-25). Oswald Chambers writes, "It is by the heart that God is perceived [known] and not by reason...so that is what faith is: God perceived by the heart." This is why God tells us in Proverbs 4:23, "Above all else, guard your heart, for it is the wellspring of life." He knows that to lose heart is to lose everything. Sadly, most of us watch the oil level in our car more carefully than we watch over the life of our heart.[8]

We must desire God's Word, long to speak with him, be excited about loving people, loving worship and loving the weak. We need a consuming **LOVE**.

Not the Easier Road, But the Right Road

The Road Not Taken[9]
–Robert Frost

Two roads diverged in a yellow wood,
And sorry I could not travel both
And be one traveler, long I stood
And looked down one as far as I could
To where it bent in the undergrowth;
Then took the other, as just as fair,
And having perhaps the better claim,
Because it was grassy and wanted wear;
Though as for that the passing there
Had worn them really about the same,
And both that morning equally lay
In leaves no step had trodden black.
Oh, I kept the first for another day!
Yet knowing how way leads on to way,
I doubted if I should ever come back.
I shall be telling this with a sigh
Somewhere ages and ages hence:

> Two roads diverged in a wood, and I,
> I took the one less traveled by,
> And that has made all the difference.

A consuming love takes more effort than a checklist. Which is tougher?

- To read your Bible for twenty minutes or to hide God's Word in your heart?
- To pray for 30 minutes or to pray without ceasing?
- To meet a new person every week or to love your neighbor as yourself?
- To show up at worship for two hours on Sunday or to present your body as a living sacrifice?

To put your heart into something is much more challenging than going through a checklist.

We must look for God outside a checklist—outside the box. To love God requires heart and desire. Curtis and Eldredge write:

> Indeed, if we will listen, a Sacred Romance calls to us through our heart every moment of our lives. It whispers to us on the wind, invites us through the laughter of good friends, reaches out to us through the touch of someone we love. We've heard it in our favorite music, sensed it at the birth of our first child, been drawn to it while watching the shimmer of a sunset on the ocean. The Romance is even present in times of great personal suffering: the illness of a child, the loss of a marriage, the death of a friend. Something calls to us through experiences like these and rouses an inconsolable longing deep within our heart, wakening in us a yearning for intimacy, beauty, and adventure….
>
> The true story of every person in this world is not the story you see, the external story. The true story of each person is the journey of his or her heart.[10]

Where Do We Find God?

1 Kings 18 and 19 are chapters of great contrast. In 1 Kings 18, Elijah the prophet challenges the prophets of Baal to a contest, and he wins a great battle for God by standing up to the prophets of

Baal. In chapter 19, Queen Jezebel sends word to Elijah that he is in a heap of trouble and has one day to live. Instead of standing up to the Queen, Elijah flees to the south and hides in a cave. The word of the Lord comes to Elijah while he is in the cave and asks him, "Why are you here?" Elijah protests that he has been very zealous for God, but that zeal has gotten him in deep trouble. Then the Lord told Elijah to go out of the cave and stand on the mountain, and he (the Lord) was to pass in front of him.

What would God look like? Where would his presence reside? Like Elijah, most of us would expect to see God in the wind, the earthquake or the fire.

1 Kings 19:11-12 reads:

> The Lord said, "Go out and stand on the mountain in the presence of the Lord, for the Lord is about to pass by."
>
> Then a great and powerful wind tore the mountains apart and shattered the rocks before the Lord, but the Lord was not in the wind. After the wind there was an earthquake, but the Lord was not in the earthquake. After the earthquake came a fire, but the Lord was not in the fire. And after the fire came a gentle whisper. When Elijah heard it, he pulled his cloak over his face and went out and stood at the mouth of the cave."

God isn't found in the wind, the earthquake or the fire. He is present in the "quiet whisper." My Hebrew professor, James Durham, said that the Hebrew behind the phrase "quiet whisper" could be translated, "a silence that was so silent that it could be heard." God was there in the silence. Those who follow the way of the heart find God in the most unexpected places.

Where can we find God? In many varied places:

- in silence
- in a wonderful novel
- by walking in the woods or sitting in the sun
- by playing with a child
- by reading poetry
- by writing in a journal
- by listening to music
- by taking a nap
- by staring at a baby

- by talking to a friend
- by helping a neighbor
- by trying something new
- by living in the moment
- by meditating on the Bible
- by working in your garden
- by holding hands with a loved one
- by looking up at the stars
- by watching the clouds pass by
- by eating a Krispy Kreme donut
- by watching a football game
- by looking at a photo album
- by taking care of a sick child
- by losing security
- by struggling with the death of a loved one
- by being still before the Lord
- by being consumed by God

God is in everything. He is a part of everything we do. We must develop a consuming love for him.

Conclusion

When asked what is the greatest commandment, Jesus answered, "Love the Lord your God with all your heart, soul, mind and strength." This means that we must be consumed by our love for God.

We must redefine our love for God. I'm going to start by seeing it as a romance. Instead of "ought to love God," I'm going "to desire to love him." Instead of "do, do, do," I'm going to "be, be, be." Instead of a checklist, I'm going to focus on a relationship. Let's have a consuming love for God and love him with all our heart, soul, mind and strength. Ask yourself, "Do you **LOVE** God?"

Dearest Abba,

Show me your **LOVE** so that I may learn to **LOVE** you with a **LOVE** that has no bounds, no conditions, no limits, no qualifications, no quantifications, no barriers, no restrictions, no boundaries and no borders. I desire to **LOVE** you with an absolute, unconditional, unreserved, unrestricted, *agape* **LOVE**.

In Jesus name
Amen

Endnotes

1 Eugene H. Peterson, *The Message* (Colorado Springs: NavPress, 2002), 2223-2224.
2 Fenelon, 81.
3 Mulholland, *Invitation to a Journey*, 89.
4 France, 319.
5 Carson, 495.
6 Gilbert K. Chesterton, Heretics, 12th edition. (Norwood, Mass.: Plimpton Press), Chapter XIV "On Certain Modern Writers and the Institution of the Family." http://www.bibleteacher.org/here7.htm (accessed March 22, 2006.)
7 Oswald Chambers, *My Utmost For His Highest* (Westwood, N.J.: Dodd Mead & Company, Inc., 1935), 112.
8 Curtis and Eldredge, *The Sacred Romance* (Nashville: Thomas Nelson, 1997), 9.
9 Robert Frost, Mountain Interval, New York: Henry Holt and Company, 1920; Bartleby.com. 1999. http//www.bartleby.com/119/. (accessed March 22, 2006).
10 Ibid, 6-7.

Chapter Ten

The Second Greatest Command

When we review Matthew 22:34-41, Mark 12:28-31, and Luke 10:25-28, we see that Jesus didn't just answer the question about the greatest commandment and stop there. He went on to add that there was a second great commandment—to love your neighbor as yourself. As far as we know, Jesus is the only rabbi to tack this second commandment onto the first one. The first commandment was "Hear, Oh Israel, the Lord, your God, is one God and love the Lord your God with all your heart, soul, mind, and strength." The second commandment was like unto it, "Love your neighbor as yourself." The first commandment was taken from Deuteronomy 6:4-5. The second commandment comes from Leviticus 19:18. Jesus not only added the second commandment to the first, he also noted that on these two commandments all the Law and the Prophets hang.

WHY IS THIS IMPORTANT?

Why is it important that Jesus on his own initiative adds the second commandment to the first? Because Jesus demonstrates that our love for God must be translated into a love for people. This has always been a failing in religion—think of the Pharisees, the Judaizers, the Gnostics, the Catholic church of the Dark Ages, down to our own day. We cannot claim to love God unless we love people.

1 John 4:20-21 reads, "If anyone says, 'I love God,' yet hates his brother, he is a liar. For anyone who does not love his brother, whom he has seen, cannot love God, whom he has not seen. And he has given us this command: Whoever loves God must also love his brother." To love God means that we must love people.

We also see the importance of linking these two commands when Jesus says, "All the Law and the Prophets hang on these two commandments." That is like saying, "everything depends on this." D.A. Carson notes:

> These two commandments are the greatest because all Scripture 'hangs' on them; i.e., nothing in Scripture can cohere or truly be obeyed unless these two are observed. The entire biblical revelation demands heart religion marked by total allegiance to God, loving him and loving one's neighbor. Without these two commandments the Bible is sterile.[1]

This has been proven true throughout the history of the church. If we don't have a consuming love for God and an unconditional/serving love for people (people both inside and outside the church)—everything will fall apart. We can have many other aspects of the Gospel in good working order—proper doctrine, total commitment, true sacrifice, biblical discipleship—but if we fail in loving God and loving neighbor—everything will come to a grinding halt. God will place his hand of discipline on us. It is like trying to drive your car without ever changing the oil. You can run for a while on old, used oil. You might be able to push the car 5,000 miles or 7,000 miles, but at some point you will begin to notice problems. If you keep pushing the car, then the car will come to a halt. You will burn out the engine. Loving God and loving people is the oil in the engine of the church. Without this oil, the church can make some advances; but eventually everything will come to a grinding halt.

In Matthew's gospel, Jesus answers the scribe's question concerning the greatest commandment just before he rebukes the Pharisees in chapter 23. This context is important because the Pharisees believed they were experts at keeping the law and honoring the prophets. They equated loving God with keeping the law (See Matthew 23:23-26 and Matthew 23:29-32). When we push to keep the commands of God without remembering our love for people, we are Pharisees. Loving God and loving people must appear in our lives simultaneously.

Consider the Example of Jesus

Jesus loved God and he loved people. We see Jesus' concern for people in Matthew 9:35-38:

> Jesus went about all the cities and villages teaching in their synagogues and proclaiming the good news of the kingdom

> and healing every disease and every sickness. When he saw the crowds he had compassion on them because they were harassed and helpless as sheep without a shepherd. Then he said to his disciples, "The harvest is plentiful, but the workers are few. Therefore ask the Lord of the harvest to send workers into his harvest.[2]

I've read this verse often while focusing on the ministry of Jesus. I've emphasized that Jesus was going, teaching, preaching, healing and praying. I've also taught that Jesus was doing this because he wanted a harvest. His sacrifice was all about the harvest. But I overlooked the real reason why he was doing those things—he had compassion on people. Jesus loved people deeply. That is why he went, taught, preached, healed and prayed. He saw the crowds and he had compassion for them. He saw the crowds and his heart went out to them because they were harassed and helpless, like sheep without a shepherd.

The going, teaching, preaching, healing, and praying must come from our compassion for people. Leadership guru, John C. Maxwell, writes in his book *Be A People Person*:

> Jesus went, saw, felt and cared. It's only when we go and expose ourselves to various situations that we will see enough to develop the concern necessary to move us to action.
>
> It's difficult to become motivated to help people without first seeing and feeling their needs. The secret is to spend time with them. Only when you go and see will you feel and do.[3]

Do we love people? Do we love people the way Jesus did? Do we love enough to go to them, see their need, feel their hurt and care for them? This is how Jesus loved. He was moved by compassion for people. He loved God, and he loved people.

The Three Aspects of the Second Commandment

When you break down the command, "Love your neighbor as yourself," there are three aspects to this commandment. Let's take a look at these three aspects.

Love

This word, *agapaseis*, is from the Greek work, *agape*, which is the same word that was used to describe our love for God in the first commandment. It is an unconditional love—a love without limits. *Agape* is a consuming love. It is not the lower case "love," but it is capital letters "**LOVE**." It is heart, passion and service. We should take the same love that we have for God and translate that into a love for people. We must **LOVE** people with the same **LOVE** that we have for God.

This love is described by Jesus in John 15:9-17. Jesus instructs us to "love each other as I have loved you." He not only tells us to love each other, but he qualifies that love by adding, "as I have loved you." In the way that God, Jesus and the Holy Spirit love us, we are now to love others.

What is involved in this type of *agape* love?

- We must be willing to lay down our lives for each other.
- We must love each other as Jesus has loved us.
- We must be careful, attentive and active in listening to each other.
- We must want the best for each other.
- We must make sure that we are meeting the other person's needs.
- We must be there for each other in the good times and in the bad.
- We must make sure that everyone feels needed and important—that no one is left out and that no one is a castaway.
- We must be able to express ourselves openly and honestly without feeling put down, shut down or belittled.
- We must make our fellowship safe.

What is this *agape* **LOVE** that we are to demonstrate to others? John Powell, a professor and counselor, writes that the message of unconditional love is:

> The essential message of unconditional love is one of liberation: you can be whoever you are, express all your thoughts and feelings with absolute confidence. You do not have to be fearful that love will be taken away. You will not be punished for your openness or honesty. There is no admission

> price to my love, no central fees or installment payments to be made. There may be days when disagreements and disturbing emotions may come between us. There may be times when psychological or physical miles may lie between us. But I have given you the word of my commitment. I have set my life on a course. I will not go back on my word to you. So feel free to be yourself, to tell me all of your negative and positive reactions, of our warm and cold feelings. I cannot always predict my reaction or guarantee my strength, but one thing I do know and I do want you to know: I will not reject you! I am committed to your growth and happiness.[4]

We need to feel loved because we get so beat up by the world. We need a safe haven, a place of security. We need people who are going to build us up and not tear us down. We need friends who will build our confidence and love us for who we are and not just for what we do. We need unconditional love.

When I was a boy growing up in Columbia, Tennessee, my family always had dogs around the house. We were dog people, not cat people. I never remember us buying a dog. We either went to the pound or we took in a stray from around the neighborhood. In fact, one dog we named Tramp because that's what he was—a tramp. If you've ever been around a stray dog, they are often jumpy and easily scared and agitated. They often shake when around people because they don't trust people. They are use to being "shooed" along and talked down to. They have had rocks and sticks thrown at them. They've heard people say, "get away," "go on, dog, get out of here" or "scram."

But when you take in a stray dog, they learn to become confident. They stop shaking and start taking. That's right, they start taking over the whole house. They get bold. You might see them on your bed or on your sofa. Once they feel safe, they feel free to be themselves.

In this way, people aren't much different from dogs. The world has treated us like strays. We've been bitten, chewed up and spit out. The church should be a safe haven. Unconditional love is an accepting love. Only when we feel safe, do we will feel free to be ourselves.

Neighbor

We are to love our neighbor. The question naturally arises: Who is my neighbor? Many Jews of Jesus' day had developed a selective "love" that was meant only for those within their covenant community. In fact, they had added to the law that it was okay to hate their enemies. Jesus teaches against this in Matthew 5:43-48. Jesus makes it clear that we are to love neighbor and enemy.

Our neighbor is anyone:

- who hands you your dry cleaning
- who delivers your mail
- who coaches your child in soccer
- who walks past you on a sidewalk
- who honks his or her horn at you at the traffic light
- who is homeless
- who has a mansion
- with a different accent
- who smells funny at the end of the day
- who walks with a limp
- who talks with a lisp
- who is a complete stranger
- who is your best friend
- who is just like you
- who is worlds apart from you

We are to have an *agape* love for everyone.

Obviously we can't be super close to everyone. Even Jesus had his chosen twelve with whom he spent more focused time than with anyone else. And out of those twelve, he had the three—Peter, James and John—that he singled out for specific training. But Jesus loved everyone. He had a way of making everyone feel accepted and included.

Too often, our nature can be to run in a pack and form cliques that exclude other people. As I said before, it is natural to be closer to some people and form deeper relationships with a few than with many. We need those close relationships. But we must guard against forming cliques that shut out our neighbors.

Yourself

How can you love your neighbor as yourself if you harbor self-hatred in your heart? Love includes learning to love self. The older I get the more I realize that we all have our little quirks and failings. None of us is perfect. In some way we are all cracked. We all have our flaws. But God doesn't except us to be perfect. He accepts our imperfections. We have to learn to accept our imperfections as well.

Perhaps you have heard the story that comes from India entitled, "The Cracked Pot."[5] A servant used two pots every day to bring water from the river to his master's home. One pot was perfect. The other pot was had a slight crack in its upper half. Every day the water-bearer would strap the two pots to either end of a pole and carry the pole across his shoulders to retrieve water from the river. He would fill each pot to the brim, but by the time the pots reached the house the pot with the crack would be half-empty.

The pot with the crack felt terrible and inadequate because it showed up at the house every day only half-full. It always compared itself to the perfect pot. The perfect pot would arrive at the house filled with water, fulfilling its purpose as a vessel for transporting water. The cracked pot grew frustrated over its imperfection. One day it voiced it frustration to the servant, saying, "I'm sorry that I'm cracked. I feel like I'm such a burden to you because every day you fill me with water to the brim and every day I arrive at the house half empty."

The servant looked down at the pot and replied, "No, you shouldn't feel that way at all. That small crack in your frame allows only a small amount of water to leak out at a time. I've used that crack to water seeds that I have sprinkled on your side of the path. Notice the flowers on your side of the path. These flowers have been watered by the slow leak from this crack. Without you, these flowers would not have grown. I cut these flowers and place them on the master's table. It is because of you that our master gets fresh flowers every day."

In some way, we are all cracked. Every single one of us has flaws. The key is to realize that God accepts our flaws and will use our flaws to bring greater glory to him. Paul had a thorn in the flesh. He begged God to take it away, but God said no. God told Paul, "My grace is sufficient for you." Paul had to learn to accept his thorn. God accepted Paul with his thorn. Paul had to learn to accept his thorn.

Anything that helps us see our need for God is a blessing.

We all need acceptance. But the biggest place we need acceptance is in our own hearts. Once we accept ourselves even with cracks, we can learn to accept other people even with their flaws and cracks. To **LOVE** our neighbor, we must learn to **LOVE** ourselves. This is an important aspect of the second great command.

Dear Father in Heaven,

Thank you for your unconditional **LOVE**. Please help me to be a conduit of your *agape* **LOVE** to my neighbor. Help me to see that everyone is my neighbor. People I like, and people I don't like. People who like me, and people who don't like me. People that I am like, and people that I am nothing like. They are all my neighbor. And help me to **LOVE** myself. Help me to accept my flaws, my cracks, my quirks, my shortcomings and my failures in the same way that you accept them. And help me to understand that your grace is sufficient for me.

In your son Jesus' name
Amen

Endnotes

1 Carson, 465.

2 The author's own translation.

3 John C. Maxwell, *Be A People Person* (Colorado Springs: Victor Books, 1994), 27.

4 John Powell, *Unconditional Love* (Niles, Illinois: Argus Communications, 1978), 67-68.

5 Story found in Manning's *A Ruthless Trust.*

Part Five

Character Studies on the Heart

Look at every path closely and deliberately, then ask ourselves this crucial question: Does this path have a heart? If it does, then the path is good. If it doesn't, it is of no use.
–Carlos Castañeda, American Anthropologist and mystic

In every man there is something wherein I may learn of him, and in that I am his pupil.
–Ralph Waldo Emerson, American poet

Chapter Eleven

A Man After God's Own Heart–The Heart of David

"A man after God's own heart." Imagine having that phrased tattooed on your forehead to carry with you throughout life. But that is exactly what was said about Israel's second king, the shepherd king, David son of Jesse. One of the most valuable lessons that we learn from a study of David's life is that to be a person after God's own heart doesn't mean you have to be perfect. David was far from perfect. He wasn't a perfect person, a perfect king or a perfect father. David was flawed like all of us are flawed. No one is perfect. We can't walk a perfect walk. But we can, in spite of our imperfections, continually acknowledge the perfection of God. David did this. Even when he messed up, he admitted his mistakes and acknowledged that he sinned against God. The psalms he wrote are a testimony to his heart. They stand today as a tribute to a man who longed to find new and lasting ways to praise the greatness of God.

We can learn many lessons from the life of David. We can learn what it means to be "a person after God's own heart."

A Trusting Heart

David Trusted God's Authority: A Song and a Harp

When David was selected to serve in Saul's court, it was for a specific reason. King Saul was crazy. He was certifiable. David's music calmed King Saul. So David was selected to be a court musician for the king. 1 Samuel 16:14-22 tells the story, "Now the Spirit of the Lord had departed from Saul, and an evil spirit from the Lord tormented him." Leaving God can drive us crazy. "Saul's attendants said to him, 'See an evil spirit from God is tormenting you. Let our Lord command his servants here to search for someone who can play the harp. He will play when the evil spirit from God comes upon you, and you will feel better." Saul's advisors suggest that music can calm the savage beast. They searched for a court musician to play the harp whenever Saul had an attack. So Saul said to his attendants, "Find someone who plays well and bring him to me." King Saul agreed with the idea. He ordered his advisors to make it happen. One of the servants answered, "I have seen a son of Jesse of Bethlehem who knows how to play the harp. He is a brave man and a warrior. He speaks well and is a fine-looking man. And the Lord is with him." Notice how impressed the servant was with David. David had many great characteristics and attributes. But the most important characteristic about David, the servant saved for last—"And the Lord is with him." So Saul sent for David. Saul liked David and asked Jesse, David's father, to allow David to stay in his service. David became a court musician and an armor-bearer for King Saul.

David must have had mixed feeling about this. He got to play his harp and compose songs for the King of Israel, but the king was crazy. It was now David's job to soothe the king. Whenever an evil spirit entered the king, David would play his harp and the evil spirit would leave. Saul would then feel better. David had firsthand experience of the declining spiritual and mental health of King Saul. And yet, he continued to respect Saul. David continued to try to help the king whenever he had an attack. He trusted that God would work through the situation.

Although the relationship between David and Saul started amiably, Saul soon grew bitter toward David. After David killed Goliath in battle, the people began to sing the praises of David. They danced and sang, "Saul has killed his thousands, and David his tens of thousands" (1 Samuel 18:7). This infuriated Saul. He grew jealous of David. He grew afraid of David's success. He made David his enemy.

But David continued to serve Saul faithfully. He fought battles and gave the honor to Saul. He continued to play the harp for Saul. David trusted that God would make things right. He saw Saul as God's anointed and respected the kingship of Saul.

Saul's jealousy and hatred of David continued to grow. It grew to the point that Saul took a spear and attempted to kill David. David had to flee for his life. Later, Saul killed 85 priests who were loyal to David. Saul pursued David throughout the wilderness of Judea to try to arrest him and kill him. David became "public enemy #1" in Saul's eyes. Saul did everything in his power to track down David and put him to death.

How did David respond to Saul? He didn't retaliate. He tried to stay one step ahead of the king in order to outrun him. When David had a chance to kill King Saul, he didn't do it. He would not kill the Lord's anointed (1 Samuel 24:8-13). David trusted God's authority. God was getting David ready to be king. We can't always see or understand how God is working in our lives. But he is always working on us.

David Trusted God's Power: A Sling and a Stone

David learned many lessons about God's power by studying nature when he was a shepherd of his father's sheep just outside of Bethlehem. The psalms are filled with images from nature that express the power of God. David learned to trust God's power. The story of David begins in 1 Samuel 16. Samuel, the last judge of Israel, visited Jesse of Bethlehem in order to anoint one of Jesse's sons as the next king of Israel. Jesse paraded all of his sons in front of Samuel except one; he forgot about his youngest son David who was out in the fields watching over the sheep. So Samuel asked Jesse, "Don't you have any other sons? God has not chosen any of the sons that you have shown me." Jesse sent for David. About another son, God instructed Samuel, "Do not consider his appearance or his height, for I have rejected him. The Lord does not look at the things man looks at. Man looks at the outward appearance, but the Lord looks at the heart" (1 Samuel 16:7). God saw the heart of David, and selected David to be the next king of Israel.

Samuel anointed David as King. When he anointed David, the Scripture says, "From that day on the Spirit of the Lord came upon David in power" (1 Samuel 16:13). David trusted in God's power. Because David trusted in God's power, he was able to defeat the Philistine champion, Goliath, in battle (1 Samuel 12). Goliath came out every day to make fun of God's army. He challenged them by saying, "I defy the ranks of Israel." He did this for forty days. David heard the challenge and asked, "Who is this uncircumcised Philistine that he should defy the armies of the living God?" David accepted Goliath's challenge. He took the weapons of a shepherd—a staff, five small stones and a slingshot. A shepherd against the warrior champion of the Philistine army. But David had a warrior's heart. A warrior's heart that trusted in the power of God. And God's power came through for David. 1 Samuel 17:50 reads, "So David triumphed over the Philistine with a sling and a stone; without a sword in his hand he struck down the Philistine and killed him." A sling and a stone. Remember this image. It is an image that reminds us to trust in God's power.

God's power, the same power that led David to triumph over Goliath, is available to all of us today. We still have Goliaths in our lives. Philistine giants who try to get us to doubt the power of God. Philistine giants who mock us and ridicule our decision to trust in God's power. Today our sling and our stone is repentance. Repentance gives us the power to change and to cast off the Goliaths in our lives. In Luke 13:3-5, Jesus tells his followers, "Repent or perish." Through repentance God makes his power to change available to us.

In Revelation 3:19-20, Jesus gives us an invitation. He says, "Those whom I love I rebuke and discipline. So be earnest, and repent. Here I am! I stand at the door and knock. If anyone hears my voice and opens the door, I will come in and eat with him, and he with me."

How do you feel when you need to repent? Do you feel fear, shame, overwhelming anxiety or hopelessness? Trust in God's power to change your life. After you repent, you will feel differently. Acts 3: 19-20 reads, "Repent, then and turn to God, so that your sins may be wiped out that times of refreshing may come from the Lord, and that he may send the Christ, who has been appointed for you—even Jesus." Jesus is there when we repent. God wipes away our sins. Times of refreshing come.

Have you ever had to go days without taking a bath or a shower? Perhaps you were in a terrible storm and your water supply was cut off. Perhaps you were camping in the wilderness. Perhaps you were too sick to tolerate a bath or shower. If so, you know the feeling of having greasy, matted hair. You know the feeling of having oily skin with a layer of dirt on top. You know the odor that lingers no matter how many sponge baths you give yourself. After days without a bath, how refreshing that first real bath with soap, shampoo and running water feels. That is the feeling of genuine repentance.

But what is genuine, real repentance? It is more than just

feeling sorry about something. It's more than feeling badly because you got caught doing something. It implies lasting change. In 2 Corinthians 7: 8-13, Paul defines repentance:

> But your sorrow led you to repentance. For you became sorrowful as God intended and so were not harmed in any way by us. Godly sorrow brings repentance that leads to salvation and leaves no regret, but worldly sorrow brings death. See what this godly sorrow has produced in you: what earnestness, what eagerness to clear yourselves, what indignation, what alarm, what longing, what concern, what readiness to see justice done. At every point you have proved yourselves to be innocent in this matter.

That is true, genuine repentance.

What is your Goliath? Perhaps laziness or cowardice or selfishness? Maybe lust or greed or jealousy? Could it be hatred or prejudice or racism? Maybe it is gossip or lying or slander? Maybe it is immorality or debauchery or impurity? Perhaps it is discord, fits of rage or drunkenness? There are plenty of Goliaths to go around. When one dies, another takes the field.

The real question that I have for you is—where are your sling and stone? God's power is available to you to defeat your Goliaths. The power is available through repentance. Repentance is your sling and your stone. Let's trust in God's power to overcome sin in our lives. Let's learn the lesson of a penitent heart.

A Stumbling Heart

Our newspapers are filled with tragic headlines. Here is a small sampling:

Mother in Houston Murders Her Five Children
The Prince of Nepal Shoots Parents Then Shoots Himself
50 Abducted in Iraqi Raid; 24 Bodies Found in Baghdad
Bomb in Tel Aviv Nightspot Kills 18

Perhaps you missed this one:

King of Israel Murders Loyal Military Commander after Seducing His Wife.[1]

The article following this headline reads:

Rumors were confirmed today that David son of Jesse, the king of Israel, had his military advisor, Uriah the Hittite, murdered and brought his wife, Bathsheba, into the palace as a royal concubine. Several weeks ago, this paper broke the news that Uriah the Hittite, loyal soldier and army commander, died in battle. Suspicions concerning his death grew when some soldiers reported that they were commanded to draw back from Uriah thus exposing him to a direct attack from the enemy. A military inquiry found no wrongdoing in the matter. But other questions surfaced when the King took Uriah's wife, Bathsheba, into the palace.

All questions were answered today when Nathan, a high-ranking advisor to the King gave an exclusive interview to this reporter. Nathan told the Jerusalem Star, "King David is guilty of adultery and murder. I have spoken with the King on these matters and he admits his wrongdoing. The King is sorry for his actions and wants to make amends." Nathan confirmed what the rumor mills had been circulating for weeks. We attempted to contact the King directly for comment, but were unsuccessful. The public once lauded David as being the greatest king in the entire world. After this incident, his public approval ratings are expected to plummet.

David's early life was filled with victories. It seemed that nothing would dim the brilliance of Israel's brightest star. But his star did dim. It dimmed almost to the point of going out altogether. How could David stumble from such a great height? How and why did this happen?

He Took His Eyes Off God's Mission

When we take our eyes off God's purpose and mission in life, then we are destined to stumble into the trap of sin. David was king. As king, he had specific responsibilities that fell on his shoulders. In the spring of the year, kings went to war with their armies. David knew his responsibility. He had been leading his troops into battle during the fighting season for years. Why would a warrior king stay at home and not go to battle? Perhaps he grew tired of battle. Perhaps he was enticed to stay at home and seek out his personal comfort. Perhaps he felt that he had done his part for God and country by leading in battle so many times before this. Perhaps he grew apathetic. Perhaps he became a master at delegating his responsibilities to other people. Whatever the reason, David stumbled because he took his eyes off God's mission. He failed in his purpose as king.

The maxim says, "Idle hands are the devil's workshop." To keep sin out, we must stay busy with doing what we know is right. When we take our eyes off God's mission, then we are destined to stumble into sin.

He Failed to Say "No" to Sin

2 Samuel 11:2-3 reads, "One evening David got up from his bed and walked around on the roof of the palace. From the roof he saw a woman bathing." David, stop! Just stop right there! David turn around and walk back inside your palace. Go inside and pray. Go inside and read some Scripture. Go inside and play cards with some of your guards. Go inside and take a cold shower. Just stop right there. But David doesn't stop.

The text continues, "The woman was very beautiful." David stop! Don't take a second look! Turn around and walk inside! Call for Nathan and tell him about your struggles. Stop right there. But David doesn't stop.

The text continues, "And David sent someone to find out about her." David stop! Stop right there! Don't send someone to find out about her. Control yourself. But no, now he includes others in his sin.

His guard tells him, "Isn't this Bathsheba, daughter of Eliam, the wife of Uriah the Hittite?" The man gives David an out. "Hey David, this is someone's daughter. This is someone's wife." She's married. David stop! David take the out. Tell yourself, "Oh right, she's married, what am I thinking." She is someone else's wife. End of the story. But it's not. David goes on.

The text continues, "Then David sent messengers to get her." David stop! Just stop right there! It takes some time for the messengers to go and bring her back. During that time, come to your senses. Even before she arrives at the palace, send another set of messengers to catch the first set and say, "Sorry! Big mistake! Sorry to have bothered you! Please try bathing indoors from now on!" Catch yourself before you make a tragic mistake. But David doesn't stop.

The text reads, "She came to him." Stop! Stop yourself right there! Here she is. Send her back home. You've coveted your neighbor's wife, but haven't committed adultery yet. Tomorrow, you will make a sacrifice and all will be okay. Just sent her back home. But David doesn't.

The text reads, "And he slept with her." Then come the consequences. She becomes pregnant, he attempts to conceal his sin and explain away the pregnancy by ordering Uriah back from war to sleep with Bathsheba. But Uriah is a good soldier. He refuses to sleep with his wife while the rest of the army is in the field. David's sin cannot be hidden. So he has Uriah murdered.

David had so many opportunities to say "no" to sin. But he kept going down the wrong path until it led to destruction. Dallas Willard describes our failure to say no to sin by comparing it to someone sitting on a long conveyor belt heading into a buzz saw. As you are on the conveyor belt, you see the saw from a good distance away. But instead of just stepping off the conveyor belt, you stay on it. You get closer and closer to the saw. All the while, you can step off the conveyor belt. But you sit on the conveyor belt and get ripped apart by the buzz saw.

David was on the conveyor belt for a long time before he actually hit the buzz saw of adultery. That is how sin is. We have to learn to say "No!" to sin. Before we sin, we are tempted by sin. That is the conveyor belt. On that belt, while we are being tempted, we need to say, "No!" We can jump off the conveyor belt.

Consider these scriptures:

> When tempted, no one should say, "God is tempting me.' For God cannot be tempted by evil, nor does he tempt anyone; but each one is tempted when, by his own evil desire, he is dragged away and enticed. Then, after desire has conceived, it gives birth to sin; and sin, when it is full-grown, gives birth to death (James 1:13-15).

Do you see the pattern here? We have evil desire in our hearts. Something entices that evil desire. We acquiesce to the desire. Then we sin. We must pray to rid our hearts of evil desires. But when that fails, we must guard our hearts from enticements. When that fails, we must fight against the enticements and learn to say, "No!"

> Do not love the world or anything in the world. If anyone loves the world, the love of the Father is not in him. For everything in the world—the cravings of sinful man, the lust of his eyes and the boasting of what he has and does—comes not from the Father but from the world. The world and its desires pass away, but the man who does the will of God lives forever (1 John 2:15–17).

John is very clear here. Do not love the world. The world feeds our cravings for sin. The world appeals to our eyes. The world strokes our egos. So, to say "No!" to the world means that we will cut off our sinful cravings, put blinders on our eyes to lust, and put to death our prideful egos.

> So, if you think you are standing firm, be careful that you don't fall! No temptation has seized you except what is common to man. And God is faithful; he will not let you be tempted beyond what you can bear. But when you are tempted, he will also provide a way out so that you can stand up under it (1 Corinthians 10:12–13).

If you think you are standing firm, be careful you don't fall. Stay humble. I remember a time I saw a young boy riding on a scooter beside his father. His father told the boy, "Slow down, you're going too fast." The boy looked back at his dad and said, "Oh, Dad! I'm great on this thing." Just about that time his front wheel hit a small, little twig that was in the road. The scooter stopped dead in it tracks, and the boy went flying right over the top of the scooter. "If you think you are standing firm, be careful that you don't fall."

When you feel like you are going to fall, that is a good sign. It means that you have not become over-confident. That is your protection against falling—to realize that you can fall. And when you are tempted to sin, look for the way out. God always provides the way out.

About twenty years ago, I went to Vermont with some friends to go skiing. I'm a terrible skier. I grew up in Middle Tennessee, and we didn't have any mountains and very little snow. So I didn't grow up skiing. My friends were all better skiers than I was. But in my pride, I tried to keep up with them. We went around corner, and I was going way too fast. I saw that I was not going to make the corner, so I looked for my way out. To my right was a huge tree. To my left was a huge boulder. Straight ahead was a drop of six feet into snow. I chose the snow. That was my way out. Whenever you are tempted, look for a way out. God always provides a way out. Often it is as simple as saying a little two-letter word, "No!"

All of these verses teach that when we are tempted, there is a way of escape. I hear people say, "I fell into sin." They act like sin is a well-placed land mine that we accidentally step on. Most of the time we go into sin with eyes wide open. In the story of David and Bathsheba, David had numerous opportunities to keep from sinning. Instead, he stayed on the conveyor belt and went right into the buzz saw.

A Restored Heart

Grace and Forgiveness

When I was a young boy around 7 or 8 years old, I made a mistake that I will never forget. My family was sitting around the supper table, and my father was leading the blessing. He started praying for his sick Uncle Herbert who had cancer and was about to die. He started making a noise as he was praying. I thought it was laughter. I thought that he had remembered a fond memory of Uncle Herbert—Uncle Herbert was a very funny man—and was laughing at that memory. I started to laugh with him. But then he jumped up from the supper table and stomped down the hall to the bathroom where he slammed the door behind him.

My brother punched me in the shoulder and said, "Way to go, stupid!"

I shot back, "What did I do?"

He countered, "You were laughing at his crying." I dropped my head in shame. I had never seen or heard my father cry. I thought he was laughing when he was crying. I felt like a fool.

When my father came out of the bathroom, I told him that I was sorry. I explained that I did not know he was crying. He gave me a big hug and told me it was okay. He did not cast me off. He did not take my sonship away. He restored me to his good graces. End of story. He forgave me.

But my brother kept rubbing my face in it. "Why'd you do that? You're so stupid. You can't tell the difference between crying and laughing. What's wrong with you? You're so dumb. You're an idiot."

I saw the difference between forgiveness and being beat up for a mistake. When you mess up, what do you want? Do you want forgiveness? Or, do you want someone to rub your face in it?

We will all mess up. Romans 3:23 says, "For all have sinned and fallen short of God's glory." Sin is the human condition. We will all stumble like David stumbled. But no sin has to be fatal. God is willing to forgive us and give us a second chance. He is willing to restore us to his good graces. He will even give us a restored heart. But we must see our sin, repent of our sin and ask for restoration.

How Did David Restore His Heart?

Facing Confrontation

After David sinned with Bathsheba, he needed help seeing his sin. He was blind to the evil that he had done. He had stolen another man's wife, ordered the husband's execution and was blind to his sin. He needed someone to show him the truth. But who would stand up to the King?

Enter Nathan.

Nathan was one of David's court prophets. David probably had several court prophets. The court prophet was to declare God's Word to the king regardless of the king's mood or disposition.

But notice that Nathan used wisdom as he approached David. He knew that to walk right up to David and condemn his actions would get nowhere. So he comes in through the side door. He tells David a parable about a rich man who had many sheep and a poor man who had one ewe lamb. A traveler comes to the rich man's house, and the rich man is compelled to kill a sheep and feed the traveler. But instead of killing one of his own sheep, he steals the poor man's lamb and serves it up for dinner. Upon hearing this story, David was livid. He wanted to punish the rich man for his hard-heartedness.

Nathan looks at David and says, "You are the man."

David needed help seeing his sin. At times, we all need help seeing our sin. When we can't see past our pride to admit our mistakes, we need someone who will intervene and help us see what we have done wrong. We need a Nathan in our lives. We need someone who will confront us when we sin. We need someone who is wise enough to know when to come in through the back door to get at our hearts. Whether they enter through the front door, the back door or the side door, we do need friends that will help us see our sin.

Through Cleansing Confession

Once David understood what he had done, it hit him hard. 2 Samuel 12:13 records his reaction, "I have sinned against the Lord." He confessed his sin. He admitted his mistake.

Notice what David does in his confession to the Lord--he calls sin, "sin." He doesn't dress it up. He doesn't blame shift. He doesn't mince words. He calls it as it is, "I have sinned." And, he acknowledges whom he hurt the most—the Lord.

We are not very good at confession. We have a hard time admitting our mistakes. We are taught from an early age to shift the blame to someone else. We learn how to excuse our sins. We dress up the word "sin" and try to make it more palatable by calling it a mistake, a shortcoming, a blunder, a bad habit or character flaw.

When you were young, did you ever break something while you were playing in the house? I remember a time when my brother and I were passing a football in the house. We knew we weren't allowed to do that. I don't remember if it was a bad throw or a blown reception, but someone messed up and the ball hit my Mom's favorite lamp and it broke. My Mom heard the crash and came running into the room. She saw her lamp lying in pieces on the floor.

"What happened?" she screamed.

My brother and I just looked at each other. Then one of us spoke up, "It fell."

"How did it fall?" Mom shouted.

"It just fell," we said.

"Lamps just don't fall," she said.

Then my brother looked at me and I looked at him and we both pointed at each other and said, "It was his fault."

Mom saw the football lying on the floor. There was her answer. Neither my brother nor I wanted to accept blame for the lamp. Both of us should have admitted our mistake. But neither wanted to accept blame.

When we sin, we need to confess our sin to God. He is ready to forgive us, but we must admit our mistake. That is the path to a restored heart.

Accepting the Consequences

Sin has consequences. After we see our sin and acknowledge our sin, we must be ready to deal with the consequences of our sin. For David, one consequence of his sin was that the child born to Bathsheba would die. This happened as the Lord predicted. After his son's death, David accepted the death as a consequence of his sin. He had to face the consequences of his sin for God to restore his heart.

God is always willing to forgive us. But even as he forgives us, we must realize that there might be lifelong consequences to our sins. To truly have a restored heart, we must be willing to deal with the consequences of our sins. We must be willing to approach people that we have wronged and say, "I'm sorry." We must be willing to make restitution when we have stolen or damaged something. If you have a problem with drugs or alcohol, you must be willing to go to rehab and get clean. Each sin has its on consequences. We must deal with the consequences of each sin.

Psalm 51 stands as a testimony to David's penitent heart and how God restored David's heart after he repented. It reads:

> Have mercy on me, O God,
> According to your unfailing love;
> According to your great compassion
> Blot out my transgressions.
> Wash away all my iniquity
> And cleanse me from my sin.
> For I know my transgressions,
> And my sin is always before me.
> Against you, and you only, have I sinned
> And done what is evil in your sight,
> So that you are proved right when you speak
> And justified when you judge.

Surely I was sinful at birth,
  Sinful from the time my mother conceived me.
Surely you desire truth in the inner parts;
  You teach me wisdom in the inmost place.

Cleanse me with hyssop, and I will be clean;
  Wash me, and I will be whiter than snow.
Let me hear joy and gladness;
  Let the bones you have crushed rejoice.
Hide your face from my sins
  And blot out all my iniquity.

Create in me a pure heart, O God,
  And renew a steadfast spirit within me.
Do not cast me from your presence
  Or take your Holy Spirit from me.
Restore to me the joy of your salvation
  And grant me a willing spirit, to sustain me.
Then I will teach transgressors your ways,
  And sinners will turn back to you.
Save me from blood guilt, O God,
  The God who saves me,
  And my tongue will sing of your righteousness.
O Lord, open my lips,
  And my mouth will declare your praise.
You do not delight in sacrifice, or I would bring it;
  You do not take pleasure in burnt offerings.
The sacrifices of God are a broken spirit;
  A broken and contrite heart,
O God, you will not despise.

Dear Father,

Help me to be a person after your own heart. I pray that I may have a deeper trust in you. Help me to walk with humble confidence in you. Help me to keep this relationship with you strong until the day I die. I pray that you will give me the conviction to flee from sin. When temptation comes my way, help me to look for a way out. When I stumble, help me to see my sin and to have a penitent heart. Keep me close to your breast. Guard my heart.

In his name
Amen

Endnotes

1 See 2 Samuel 11:14-17.

Chapter Twelve

The Heart of the Pharisees

At the very end of Robert Pirsig's *Zen and the Art of Motorcycle Maintenance*,[1] the author presents a conversation that occurs between a son and his father after they have traveled across the United States on a motorbike. The conversation goes like this:

> Son: "Dad, can I have a motorcycle when I get old enough?"
> Father: "If you take care of it."
> Son: "What do I have to do?"
> Father: "Lots of things. You've been watching me."
> Son: "Will you show me all of them?"
> Father: "Sure!"
> Son: "Is it hard?"
> Father: "Not if you have the right attitudes. It's having the right attitudes that is hard."

Having the right attitudes is hard. And this is one reason why so many people don't work on their attitudes. It is just so much easier to do something without having to think about the attitude behind the act. Doing is easy. Being is challenging.

We turn now in our study to look at a first-century Jewish sect–the Pharisees. Jesus directed some of his most severe rebukes to the Pharisees. The Pharisees followed the road of legalistic righteousness. They did not travel the way of the heart. As we look at the Pharisees, we can see the difference between following the way of legalism verses following the way of the heart.

Who were the Pharisees?

The Pharisees were the largest and most influential religious sect in first-century Judaism, numbering 6,000 in Judea. The word

Pharisee means "separate or separated one." The Pharisees felt they were to be separate from the rest of Judaism. They became separate by inventing a strict oral tradition of legalistic codes that had to be rigorously observed by those within their circle. Keeping these laws kept them pure. Anyone who didn't keep these laws was impure.

The Pharisees placed great emphasis on their oral traditions. Their oral traditions began for a good reason. Their goal was to build a hedge around the law so that the law would never be broken. They believed that on Sinai God gave Moses a written code—the Ten Commandments. But they also believed that God gave Moses an oral code—a body of rules that Moses passed on to Joshua and then to the Elders, Prophets and the men of the Temple. The Pharisees were the Keepers of the Traditions—this fictitious, oral law that God gave to Moses on Sinai.

During the days of Jesus there existed two leading schools among the Pharisees. Hillel led the moderate school and Shammai led the conservative school. These groups basically agreed with each other, but there were small areas of disagreement. One area of disagreement centered on divorce. Hillel approved of divorce saying a man could divorce his wife for any reason including burning breakfast. Shammai said that divorce could only occur if adultery was involved.

The Pharisees believed in a bodily resurrection after death. They also believed in angels and spirits and a punishment after death for the unrighteous. They relied upon the divine providence of God. But they ascribed undue importance to the oral law.

In summary, the Pharisees believed:

- that God controlled the lives of men
- there would be a resurrection of the body and a reward for piety
- in a world of angels and demons, a real spirit world
- that the scripture was made up of two parts: the written scripture and the oral traditions of the rabbinate

The Pharisees had their own traditions, which defined how to live a life faithful to the law. Their internal rules were sectarian with an emphasis on ritual purity, food, tithes and Sabbath observances. They were admired by the people and functioned at least some of the time as a social and political force against foreign and Hellenized Jewish leaders (i.e., those Jewish leaders who were sympathetic to Greek language and culture). Some or all were learned in the law and some were politically powerful. [2]

Who Were the Scribes?

The scribes were mostly from the sect of the Pharisees. They began as copiers of the law and advanced to become teachers of the law. They were the most educated people of the day. They knew many languages and acted as translators and stenographers.

During Jesus' day the scribe had three functions:

- theoretical development of the law from ten to 613 commandments
- teaching the law to their pupils
- pronouncing legal decisions in matters of dispute as interpreters of the law

A pupil of a scribe had two guidelines:

- to learn everything he was taught by heart
- to teach only what he had been taught and never change it

What Lessons Can We Learn by Studying the Pharisees?

An Analogy of the Heart

In our physical bodies, the heart is the muscle that pumps oxygenated blood throughout our bodies. When plaque gets on the arteries, the blood can't flow freely. This is a very serious medical condition called arteriosclerosis. It can lead to a heart attack or to a stroke. Proper diet and exercise can help keep the heart in good condition. But when too much plague forms on the arteries, serious medical procedures must be performed. A little preventive maintenance can go a long way in taking care of your physical heart.

As we have seen, the heart is the spiritual mission control center of our lives. But we need to keep our spiritual hearts in good condition. Our spiritual hearts need proper nourishment and exercise. Without proper conditioning, our spiritual hearts can get full of plaque and build-up. It can lead to a devastating spiritual condition called Pharisaic legalism. Pharisaic legalism is spiritual arteriosclerosis.

Jesus had much to say about the Pharisees and not much of it was good. The Pharisees were more concerned with form than function. They were more concerned with extrinsic motivation than intrinsic motivation. They did things because they were expected to do them.

A Study in Contrasts

Pharisaic Legalism	versus	Christian Liberty
Form	versus	Function
Doing	versus	Being
Extrinsic motivation	versus	Intrinsic motivation
Focusing on the Outer	versus	Focusing on the Inner
Performance	versus	Attitude
People-pleasing	versus	God-pleasing
Legalism	versus	Freedom
Compulsion	versus	Desire

Consider these Scriptures

Mark 7:1-23. The Pharisees were more concerned about food laws and what they put into their mouths than what came out of their minds and mouths.

Matthew 12:9-14. They were more worried about Sabbath laws and tradition than showing mercy to people on the Sabbath.

John 5:39-40. They were experts at discussing the minutia of the law, but they were blind to making the Word living and practical.

Luke 18:9-14. They went to the temple boasting of righteous acts, all the while demonstrating an unrepentant and unforgiving heart.

I don't believe the Pharisees meant to take the heart out of their religion any more than you and I would mean to have a heart attack or a stroke. We don't set about to put so much plaque on our hearts that it inhibits blood flow. But if we eat fatty foods, don't exercise and don't get medical checkups; then in time, we find ourselves walking around with a ticking time-bomb inside our chests.

The tenets of Pharisaic legalism originally had a good purpose. The Pharisees wanted to build a hedge around the law so that no one would get close to breaking the law. This isn't a bad idea. Keeping the law is an important matter (See 1 John 2:1-6). To keep from breaking a Sabbath law, the Pharisees would create a list of things that could or could not be done on the Sabbath to make sure you didn't break a Sabbath law. For example, the Law says not to work on the Sabbath. The law goes on to state that you cannot lift a burden on the Sabbath. So the Pharisees would spell out exactly what was meant by "lifting a burden" on the Sabbath. For example, if you had a cotton swab in your ear and it fell out on the Sabbath day, the Pharisees ruled that you could not lift that cotton swab up from the floor and put it back in your ear. That would be lifting a burden on the Sabbath. Nothing wrong with that helpful reminder. But over time, the helpful reminders accrued an importance equal to the Law of God. The helpful reminders became burdensome. The helpful reminders took people's eyes off the wonder of God's law. The helpful reminders became traditions and rules of men.

The Pharisees misplaced their focus. And we must realize that what we focus on in life we become. They focused on:

- not getting a divorce instead of how to make marriage great
- the ritual of hand-washing before a meal instead of having a grateful heart for what you were about to eat
- the details of temple worship instead of the heart of worship
- the external acts of giving, praying and fasting instead of the heart behind those acts
- keeping the Sabbath law instead of showing mercy to others on the Sabbath.
- the smallest details of tithing each spice and herb instead faith, justice and mercy

Jesus and the Pharisees

Jesus had much to say to the Pharisees. He condemned them for their hypocrisy. He condemned them for their hard-heartedness. Consider the seven woes against the Pharisees from Matthew 23:[3]

The First Woe
You Stand as Barriers to God's Kingdom (23:13-14)

> Woe to you, scribes and Pharisees, you hypocrites, because you shut the kingdom of heaven to men. For you do not enter nor do you allow others to enter.

In order to help people into God's kingdom, you must accept the kingdom yourself. The scribes and Pharisees were unwilling to do that. They denied that Jesus was the Messiah. They did not accept his Messianic reign. They stood outside God's kingdom. Therefore it was not possible for them to help people into God's kingdom. In this way they stood as a barrier to other people. They shut the kingdom of heaven in men's faces. Bad enough that they would not enter the kingdom themselves. Worse yet that they stood as a barrier to other people's entrance into the kingdom. This behavior warrants the first "woe" from Jesus.

The Second Woe
You Zealously Convert People to Your Oral Traditions (23:15)

> Woe to you, Scribes and Pharisees, hypocrites, you travel across land and sea to make a single convert, and when he converts you make him twice the son of hell (Gehenna) you are.

The scribes and Pharisees were mission minded. Jesus did not mind that. But they were not working to bring people into God's kingdom. They were peddling their form of Pharisaic Judaism to people. They would travel far and wide to gain one convert to their cause. They had zeal, but it was a misplaced zeal.

The Pharisees failed to see how their strict legalism was a heavy burden on the people. The people were smothering under the legalistic requirements of the Pharisees. Jesus gave this stinging condemnation: when someone becomes a convert you make him twice the son of hell you are. Their converts became even more adept at practicing the legalism of the Pharisees than their teachers. In doing so they gave up their freedom. They lost sight of mercy and grace. They lived by a self-righteous standard. Most importantly, they failed to accept Jesus as Messiah.

The Third Woe
You Are Blind Guides Who Swear False Oaths (23:16–22)

> Woe to you, blind guides, who say, "Whoever swears by the temple–it is nothing. Whoever swears by the gold of the temple--he is bound." You blind fools! Which is greater–the gold or the temple, which makes the gold sacred? You also say, "Whoever swears by the altar it is nothing, but whoever swears by the gift on the altar he is bound. You are blind. Which is greater–The gift or the altar that makes the gift sacred? Therefore whoever swears by the altar swears by it and everything on it. Whoever swears by the temple swears by it and the one who dwells in it? The one who swears by heaven swears by the throne of God and he who sits on it.

Jesus calls the Pharisees and scribes "blind guides." How can they lead people when they are blind? That is foolish. Jesus discloses an example of how they are blind guides: the swearing of oaths. The Pharisees had built a tradition that taught proper and improper ways to swear oaths or make promises. Jesus put aside this foolishness and demanded that everyone simply tell the truth (Matthew 5:33-37).

What did the Pharisees teach about the swearing of oaths? They taught that an oath had to be said in a particular fashion to be binding. To swear by the temple was not binding, but to swear by the gold of the temple was binding. To swear by the altar was not binding, but to swear by the gift of the altar was binding. You had to be a part of the circle of the Pharisees to understand these rules. Therefore, the Pharisees could easily deceive anyone outside their circle by stating an oath that was not binding. They could swear by the temple, which any non-Pharisee would think is binding since it was the most important symbol in Judaism, and the oath not be binding. If their oath was challenged, then they would explain why it was not binding: "I swore by the temple, but not the gold of the temple". This is much like the game we played as kids where if we made a promise with our fingers crossed, then the promise was void. Crossing your fingers invalidated the promise. But the Pharisees and Scribes were not children. They had established a system that was used to deceive people. They were dishonest and disingenuous.

No wonder Jesus had such hard words for them—"blind guides," "blind fools," "blind men." Jesus disclosed the foolishness of their system and turned it on its ear. He declared that the images that are truly binding are the temple, the altar and heaven. Jesus was not establishing a new system of oath-taking. He was overturning their system the same way he overturned the money tables in the temple. He had already stated his teaching on the taking of oaths in the Sermon on the Mount–don't swear. He now teaches that we should always be honest. If we do promise something, then we should follow through on our promise.

The Fourth Woe

You Neglect the More Important Matters of the Law like Justice and Mercy and Faith (23:23-24)

> Woe to you, Scribes and Pharisees, hypocrites. You tithe mint, dill, and cumin, and have neglected the more important matters of the law like justice and mercy and faith. You should do these things without neglecting the others. Blind guides, you strain at the gnat and swallow the camel.

The Old Testament law taught the practice of tithing (Deuteronomy 14:22-29). The Pharisees were keen on making sure that all of the laws on tithing were strictly enforced. Although Jesus and the early church never taught the practice of tithing, Jesus does not fault them for that practice here. He does challenge their strict adherence to tithing while showing laxity toward weightier matters of justice, mercy and faithfulness. What good does it do for you to strictly adhere to some parts of the law while neglecting other parts? What good does it do for you to strictly tithe, and then treat people harshly?

The weightier matters of the law can also be translated the "more important" matters of the law. These are matters that are closer to the heart of God. This teaching is in line with the teaching of the prophets. They taught that God desired mercy more than sacrifice. The Pharisees had gotten matters reversed. This is easy to do because it is easier to see a tithe given than it is to see mercy extended to someone. Legalism favors the physical, things that can be touched and seen. They majored in minors like hand-washing, oath-taking, and tithing. Although these things are not wrong when practiced with the right heart, the Pharisees practiced these legalistic acts while neglecting the need for justice, mercy and faithfulness.

Justice, mercy and faithfulness all have to do with how we treat other people. Tithing can be practiced without any concern for others. Justice means to treat people fairly. Mercy means to show people forgiveness. Faithfulness means to be a trustworthy person. How we treat others is central to the heart of God.

Jesus did not say that we should practice justice, mercy and faithfulness to the exclusion of tithing. We should not neglect either one. The Pharisees failed to see the heart of God. They strained at the gnat, but were choked by the camel. They would filter their wine to keep from swallowing an unclean gnat. But in treating people without justice, mercy and faithfulness, they were swallowing the camel. They had missed God's heart. In doing so they also blinded themselves to the true nature of Jesus–he was the Messiah.

The Fifth Woe

You Clean the Outside, While the Inside Stays Filthy (23:25-26)

> Woe to you, scribes and Pharisees, hypocrites, you clean the outside of the cup and plate, but inside you are full of greed and self-indulgence. Blind Pharisee! First clean the inside of the cup so that the outside may also be clean.

What was important to the Pharisees and scribes? Keeping oral traditions was important. Being seen by men was important. Practicing the externals was important. Legalism was important. They missed the importance of heart and attitude. They failed to challenge and nurture the inner person. They cleaned the outside of the cup (the externals), while the inner cup remained filthy (the heart). They kept their oral laws while their hearts were filled with greed and self-indulgence. They should have started with the heart, the inner man. They should have cleaned out the greed and selfishness. After doing this, the outside would be clean. The way to clean the outside is to clean the inside.

The Sixth Woe

You Are Whitewashed Tombs–Beautiful on the Outside, But Full of Dead Men's Bones on the Inside (23:27-28)

> Woe to you, Scribes and Pharisees, hypocrites because you are like whitewashed tombs that look beautiful on the outside, but on the inside are full of dead men's bones and all uncleanness. Thus you look righteous to men on the outside, but inside you are full of hypocrisy and wickedness.

Jesus reiterates what he just said: clean the inner man. The Scribes and Pharisees were like whitewashed tombs. Before the Passover, the Jews would whitewash the graves around Jerusalem so that they would stand out to the pilgrims traveling to the city. This way they could avoid the graves and not become ceremonially unclean. These tombs would look pretty on the outside, but inside they contained the bones of dead men.

Jesus compares the Scribes and Pharisees to these graves. This would have been particularly offensive to these leaders since Jesus was comparing them to something unclean. The religious leaders were like tombs in that they looked good on the outside, but their hearts were dead. Inside they were full of hypocrisy and wickedness. This is a devastating condemnation of the Pharisees and scribes.

The Seventh Woe

You Act as if You Would Not Have Killed the Prophets (23:29-32)

> Woe to you, Scribes and Pharisees, hypocrites, you build tombs of the prophets and decorate the graves of the righteous. You say, "If we lived in days of our fathers, we would not have taken part with them in the shedding of the blood of the prophets. Thus you testify against yourselves that you are descendants of those who murdered the prophets. And you shall fulfill the measure of the sin of your forefathers.

The Scribes and Pharisees built memorials for the prophets of the Old Testament. They did this to testify that they would not have murdered the prophets had they been living back then. But the prophets of old would have rebuked the Scribes and Pharisees just as harshly as they rebuked the false prophets of their own day. The Scribes and Pharisees were the true descendants of the people who killed the prophets. The memorial that they built stood as a testimony to their guilt. Their decision to deny Jesus as the Messiah also testified to this.

Conclusion (23:33-36)

> You snakes! You offspring of vipers! How will you flee from the condemnation of Gehenna? I am sending you prophets and wise men and teachers. Some you will kill and crucify; others you will flog in your synagogues and pursue from village to village. So on you will come all the blood of the righteous that has been shed on the earth–from the blood of righteous Abel to the blood of Zechariah son of Berekiah, whom you killed between the temple and the altar. I tell you truthfully, all this will come upon this generation.

Jesus calls the Scribes and Pharisees snakes. They are snakes and the offspring of vipers. How could they expect to escape from the condemnation of Hell? Jesus would prove that they were just like their forefathers. He would send them prophets, wise men and teachers whom they would flog and crucify. The blood of all the righteous martyrs would be on their heads, from Abel to Zechariah, from the opening to the close of the Old Testament. But the blood of the righteous would not just be on the heads of the Scribes and Pharisees. The blood would be on "this generation." In other words, anyone who follows the Scribes and Pharisees would share their fate.

What did the Pharisees do wrong? Much! Consider the following:

- They focused on external forms and not the heart.
- They focused on "the how" instead of "the why."
- They focused on doing religious acts instead of being righteous.
- They focused on performance instead of motivation.
- They preached a good message, but didn't practice it.
- They had right words, but they missed the meaning behind the words.
- They were fastidious about taking oaths properly, but unconcerned about keeping oaths.
- They gave a tithe on their spices thus keeping the smallest part of the law, but missed the important part of the law—justice, mercy and faithfulness.

- Everything they did was for men to see.

Pharisees were leaders in first century Judaism. Jesus wasn't against leadership. He was opposed to self-serving, hypocritical leadership. Leadership that serves its own self and not others is not the leadership of Jesus.

Leaves from the Notebook of a Tamed Legalist

I know firsthand the burdens of a Pharisaic approach to following God. I have been a Pharisee most of my life. I grew up in the traditional Church of Christ in Middle Tennessee where Pharisaic legalism was a way of life. Don't get me wrong, I learned some great things by growing up in the Church of Christ. I learned to love the Word of God. I learned the value of sound doctrine. I learned how to interpret the Scriptures. I learned the value of a consistent walk with God. I learned the value of godly relationships. I was saved in the traditional Church of Christ. I am thankful to God for all these things. I have a deep appreciation for my heritage and am glad that I'm a part of the Restoration Movement.

But I also learned how to be a Pharisee in the traditional Church of Christ. I'm not saying that everyone in the Church of Christ is a Pharisee. There are many great disciples in the Church of Christ. I chose to be a Pharisee. I chose to walk the path of Pharisaic legalism. Some of my Pharisaic traditions were:

- I only read out of the King James Version and the American Standard Version of the Bible. I considered every other version inaccurate.
- I believed in a strict legalistic teaching on divorce and remarriage. I believed that the only legitimate reason for divorce was adultery, and this law was to be applied to everyone inside and outside the church.
- In my prayers, I believed you had to address God by using "Thou," and "Thee," and "Thy."
- No dancing. Don't ask why; just don't do it. I often heard people say, "The dancing foot and the praying knee don't belong on the same leg."
- No drinking. Don't ask why; just don't do it. I heard people say, "One drink is one drink closer to being drunk."

- No mixed bathing. (This is the old school way of saying men and women couldn't swim in the same pool at the same time.)
- No church choirs during the worship service. (You could use a church choir for a funeral service or a wedding, but not during a church service).
- No handclapping or foot-stomping while singing in church.
- No solos for singers in church.
- No instrumental music in worship.

Then I went to a Bible college in West Tennessee called Freed-Hardeman College. I went there to study the Bible. I went because it was a very conservative school with a strong Bible department. I'm thankful for my time there. I found my wife there. I learned how to read New Testament Greek. I studied under some great professors like Rubel Shelly, William Woodson, Dowell Flatt, Porter King and Doc Woods. I became a better preacher. I became a much better Bible student. I had a great time at Freed-Hardeman College. I have fond memories of my college days. But I also continued down the road of Pharisaic legalism. I continued to embrace the Pharisaic traditions that I mentioned above. Some other Pharisaic traditions that I followed in college were:

- No facial hair for men.
- We couldn't wear shirts without collars.
- We had to go to chapel every day.
- We could *memorize* scriptures only in the King James Version or the American Standard Version of the Bible.
- There was a prayer bell in the cafeteria that went off every 20 or 30 minutes. When it sounded, you had to stop eating and bow your head while someone prayed for the food.

Later I moved to New York and became a part of the International Churches of Christ. I thought this was a move toward a more progressive group of disciples who weren't shackled with the chains of Pharisaic legalism. We did some progressive things—read from newer translations of the Bible, worshipped with instrumental music, developed a role for women in the ministry, etc. I learned some great things during my days in the International Churches of Christ.[4] I learned how to effectively study the Bible with people. I learned how to lead small group Bible discussions. I learned how to make the Bible practical and relevant. But I became mired in a deeper swamp of Pharisaic legalism than I had experienced in the traditional Church of Christ or in college. It was a different type of legalism. Instead of a doctrinal legalism, it was a behavioral legalism. Some of the Pharisaic traditions that I embraced were:

- Assignment of one-over-another discipling partners to every church member.
- Some taught that true disciples must follow the advice of their discipling partner.
- People were assigned to a Bible discussion group. Sometimes these groups were formed with great forethought; sometimes they were formed very arbitrarily.
- Everyone was expected to be at every church service, unless you were on your "deathbed."
- Everyone was expected to have a visitor at service.
- People were expected to be personally fruitful. (Personally fruitful was narrowly defined as personally meeting a person, studying the Bible with him, and baptizing him.)
- Everyone must tithe every week.
- Once a year everyone must give a "multiple" of his or her tithe to a special contribution. The church leaders decided what the multiple would be, and how the money would be spent.
- Leadership was often based on productivity and not spirituality.
- There was a policy of having only one International Church of Christ in each city. This was crystallized in the slogan, "one church, one city."
- Smaller churches were placed under larger churches, creating a hierarchy of authority.
- A small group of men called World Sector Leaders decided policy for all the churches. Often churches had no voice in policy making.

Recently we had a revolution in our churches. I believe that it was the hand of God disciplining us. Because of this, we have abandoned many of our Pharisaic tendencies. Some people were attempting to break the shackles of legalism before the revolution hit. I applaud their efforts. But I believe that it was too little too late. God took a more radical approach. He blew the roof off the house.

He forced us to shed the skin of Pharisaic legalism.

But beware—Pharisaic legalism can easily creep back into the church. Even now some want to bring back some of our old Pharisaic ways. These include:

- Stating that each church must be made up of "sold-out disciples." Then the leader of the movement gets to define exactly what "sold-out disciple" means. Thus, the leader defines who is a true Christian.
- Placing one church over another church quashing church autonomy.
- Having a leader say, "You must do ministry our way or it isn't effective ministry."
- Worse, having a leader say, "You must do ministry our way or it isn't the ministry of Jesus."
- Having to account to someone about your giving, your evangelism and your commitment.

I have lived most of my life in the swamp of Pharisaic legalism. It is a swamp that kills freedom. It is a swamp that drowns proper motivation. It is a swamp that quenches the joy of following Jesus from the heart. After many long years, I've found my way out of the swamp of Pharisaic legalism. I've been set free. I'm determined never to enter those swampy waters again.

I pray that I have not been Pharisaical in any of my comments about the traditional Church of Christ, the International Church of Christ, or what is going on in churches now. I know that it is okay to be critical of Pharisaic legalistic tendencies. It is okay because Jesus did it. The question is our heart. Are we pointing out things to help people to change, or just to be critical? I have written what I have written in hopes of helping us to steer clear of any Pharisaic traditions that might rear their ugly heads. Let's not be naïve. Pharisaical legalism is the easy road. Therefore, it is the road that many people will travel. Whole churches will be swept back into Pharisaic legalism.

Guard your own heart against it. As for me, I've decided that I will never travel down the road of Pharisaic legalism again. I ask you to pray for me. Pray that God will always show me the way of the heart and that I will keep on that path.

A Three-Letter Word that Will Drive Away Pharisaic Legalism

With the help of God, I will never be a Pharisee again. I will be a freedom fighter and fight against all legalistic, Pharisaic tendencies that I see in the church. I will never go back to old school, legalistic rules made by man. I will celebrate the freedom that I have in Christ. The freedom to worship God wholeheartedly. The freedom to say "No!" to sin because of my personal conviction. The freedom to get with anyone in the fellowship to help me be a better disciple. The freedom to evangelize my neighbors in a way that celebrates my personality. The freedom to give abundantly to the Lord without anyone else knowing how much I give. I celebrate these freedoms.

After years of being trapped in a Pharisaic swamp, I learned a little three-letter word that drives away Pharisaic legalism. It is the word, "Why?"

Ask why you are doing something. Ask why something is expected of you. Don't be afraid to ask, "Why?" To do something from the heart, you need to know the why behind the action. Why? Why? Why? Why?

One quality that separates us from animals is the ability to reflect. Refection is good. We can ask the simple question "Why?" We can step outside of the action and look at the motivation behind the action. We can look at our feelings and emotions, and we can see if our heart is engaged in the action. Henri H.M. Nouwen, theologian and spiritual writer, observed, "Reflection is essential for growth, development, and change. It is the unique power of the human person."[5] Our unique power as human beings is that we can stop and reflect on what we are doing and ask why we are doing it. When we give up that power, we give up part of our humanity.

In writing about this "unique power of the human person" called refection, Nouwen goes on to write:

> Just living life is not enough. We must know what we are living. A life that is not reflected upon isn't worth living. It belongs to the essence of being human that we contemplate our life, think about it, discuss it, evaluate it, and form opinions about it. Half of living is reflecting on what is being lived. Is it worth it? Is it good? Is it bad? Is it old? Is it new? What is it all about? The greatest joy as well as the greatest pain of living

> come not only from what we live but even more from how we think and feel about what we are living.[6]

I would add that we should not only apply what Nouwen wrote to the totality of life, but we should apply it to each and every small, daily action that makes up the totality of life. We should step out of the action and reflect on why we are doing what we are doing. Why am I sitting here reading this book? Why do I pray? Why do I talk to strangers about Jesus? Why do I do the little thing that I do every single day? Why? Why? Why?

Reflection is good.

- Why am I waking up so early on a Sunday morning, dragging my kids out of bed on one of the only days of the week that we could all sleep late, in order to drive forty-five minutes to a part of town that I normally would never visit and listen to a person who I really don't know all that well?
- Why am I spending Monday night (the only night when there is anything good on television) studying the Bible with someone who isn't a family member, isn't a close friend, isn't someone who can give me a raise at work, in fact, isn't someone that I would normally talk to except for the fact that I am now going to study the Bible with him?
- Why am I fighting traffic on a Wednesday night, skipping supper with my family, to attend a Wednesday night class at church?
- Why do I get up on a Saturday morning, drive an hour to the inner city, park my car in a dangerous neighborhood, teach a class of children I do not know and whose parents I have never met?

Just think about this: If your boss asked you to meet him at the local waffle shop at 3:00 a.m., wouldn't you ask why? Sure you would. If your Mom and your Dad unexpectedly asked you to drop by their house tomorrow after work, wouldn't you ask why? Why is a useful and powerful word.

If someone in your ministry calls a meeting at some crazy hour of the night, then ask him or her, "Why?" If a sensible response is given, then respond sensibly to the request. If he says, "because I wanted to see who is really committed to the Lord," then respectfully say, "My commitment to the Lord can't be defined in those terms." If someone asks you to fast on Saturday from sunrise to sunset, then ask, "Why?" Knowing why we do something makes all the difference.

"Why?" is a good question. Reflection is good.

For every action that we do for God, we need to know the reason behind it. Refection. So ask, "Why?" Why am I meeting this brother for coffee? Why am I giving to the contribution today? Why am I inviting this person to church? Why am I staying up late to talk to this struggling Christian? Reflect on why you are doing what you are doing. This will keep you from Pharisaic legalism. It will also help you to embrace the unique power of what makes you human. The power of reflection.

Dearest Abba,

Please, please, please, please, please don't let me get trapped in the murky swamp of Pharisaic legalism. If I start heading down that road, conk me on the head and turn me around. Teach me to ask the question, "Why?" And teach me to reflect on my action. Let me be one of your freedom fighters. Help me to stamp out Pharisaic legalism in my own heart. Form in me the heart of your Son.

In Him

Amen

Endnotes

1 Robert M. Pirsig, *Zen and the Art of Motorcycle Maintenance: An Inquiry Into Values* (Los Angeles: Audio Renaissance, 1974), Tape 6, Track 11.

2 Paul J. Achtemier, *Harper's Bible Dictionary* (San Francisco: Harper and Row, 1985), 384.

3 The translation from Matthew 23 is the author's own translation.

4 Today I consider myself as simply a minister of the gospel of Jesus. I prefer not to use any distinguishing terms like International Church Of Christ or Church Of Christ or any denominational nomenclature. I just want to be a Christian and a Christian only.

5 Nouwen, *Can You Drink the Cup*, 27.

6 Ibid.

Conclusion

The Way of the Heart

At the beginning of this book I asked you, the reader, to "imagine that you are walking alone through some dense woods on a beautiful spring day that is neither too hot nor too cold, but just the right temperature." As you walk, you stumble across two roads. One is marked, "They Way of Legalism." The other road is marked, "The Way of the Heart." The way of the heart is a difficult road. It is covered with undergrowth and the footing unsure. It takes great focus to stay on this path. But it takes us to the destination where we want to go—spiritual maturity in Christ.

The other path is popular. The other way is easy to travel. The other road is clearly marked. The other path is well trodden. But it leads to a destination where we do not wish to go—Pharisaic Legalism.

Someone said, "Your destination is determined by which path your choose." As apprentices of Jesus, let's choose to walk the way of the heart. In walking the way of the heart we are allowing God to form Christ in our hearts. In walking the way of the heart, we are following the heart of the Father, the Son and the Holy Spirit toward spiritual maturity.

Dearest Abba,

Thank you for showing us the way of the heart. Keep our feet on your path. Form Christ in us.

In your Son's name
Amen

Bibliography

Achtemier, Paul J. Editor. *Harper's Bible Dictionary*. San Francisco: Harper and Row, Publishers, Inc., 1985.

Appleton, George. General Editor. *The Oxford Book of Prayer*. Oxford: Oxford University Press, 1985.

Athanasius. *On the Incarnation*. Translated by a religious of the C.S.M.V. Crestwood, NY: St. Vladimir's Seminary Press, 1996.

Augustine. *Confessions*. New York: Penguin, 1961.

Baillie, John. *Christian Devotion*. New York: Charles Scribner's Sons, 1962.

_______. *A Diary of Private Prayer*. New York: Charles Scribner's Sons, 1949.

Baumgartel, Friedrich. "*Lev, Levah* in the OT," in the *Theological Dictionary of the New Testament*. Edited by Gerhard Kittel. Translated and Edited by Geoffrey W. Bromiley. Vol. III. Grand Rapids: Wm. B. Eerdmans Publishing Company, 1965.

Behm, Johannes. "*Kardia* in the New Testament," *Theological Dictionary of the New Testament*. Edited by Gerhard Kittel. Translated and Edited by Geoffrey W. Bromiley. Vol. III. Grand Rapids: William B. Eerdmans Publishing Company, 1956.

Bell, Martin. *Distant Fire*. San Francisco: Harper & Row, Publishers, 1986.

_______. *Nenshu and the Tiger*. New York: The Seabury Press, 1985.

_______. *Return of the Wolf*. New York: The Seabury Press, 1983.

Boa, Kenneth. *Conformed to His Image*. Grand Rapids: Zondervan, 2001.

Bonhoeffer, Dietrich. *Christ the Center*. San Francisco: Harper & Row, Publishers, 1978.

_______. *The Cost of Discipleship*. New York: Macmillan, 1963.

_______. *Creation and Fall; Temptation*. New York: Macmillan, 1974.

_______. *Life Together*. San Francisco: Harper and Row, 1954.

_______. *Selected Writings*. Edited by Edwin Robertson. London: Fount, 1985.

Brand, Paul and Yancey, Philip. *Fearfully and Wonderfully Made*. Grand Rapids: Zondervan, 1980.

_______. *In His Image*. Grand Rapids: Zondervan, 1984.

Bright, John. *The Kingdom of God*. Nashville: Abingdon, 1980.

Brown, Colin, Editor. *The New International Dictionary of New Testament Theology*. Exeter: Paternoster Press, 1975-1978.

Brother Lawrence. *The Practice of the Presence of God*. Edited by Donald E. Demaray. New York: Alba House, 1997.

Buechner, Frederick. *Brenden.* San Francisco: Harper & Row, Publishers, 1988.

_______. *The Hungering Dark.* San Francisco: Harper & Row, Publishers, 1969.

_______. *Listening to Your Life.* San Francisco: Harper SanFrancisco, 1992.

_______. *The Magnificent Defeat.* New York: The Seabury Press, 1979.

_______. *Now and Then.* San Francisco: Harper & Row, Publishers, 1983.

_______. *Peculiar Treasures: A Biblical Who's Who.* San Francisco: Harper & Row, Publishers, 1979.

_______. *A Room Called Remember: Uncollected Pieces.* San Francisco: Harper & Row, Publishers, 1984.

_______. *Son of Laughter.* San Francisco: Harper San Francisco, 1993.

_______. *Telling the Truth: The Gospel as Tragedy, Comedy, and Fairy Tale.* San Francisco: Harper & Row, Publishers, 1977.

_______. *Whistling in the Dark: An ABC Theologized.* San Francisco: Harper & Row, Publishers, 1988.

_______. *Wishful Thinking: A Theological ABC.* New York: Harper and Row, Publishers, 1973.

Bunyan, John. *The Pilgrim's Progress.* Grand Rapids: Zondervan, 1966.

Burton, Bryan. Lectures from "The Trinity in the Third Millennium." Given by Dr. Bryan Burton in the Doctor of Ministry program at Drew University, Madison, New Jersey. June 1997.

Buttrick, George Arthur. *Prayer.* New York: Abingdon-Cokesbury Press, 1962.

_______. *So We Believe, So We Pray.* New York: Abingdon-Cokesbury Press, 1951.

Carson, D.A. *The Expositor's Bible Commentary with The New International Version, Matthew.* 2 vols. Grand Rapids: Zondervan Publishing, 1995.

_______. *The Sermon on the Mount.* Grand Rapids: Baker, 1978.

Chan, Simon. *Spiritual Theology: Systematic Study of The Christian Life.* Downers Grove: InterVarsity Press, 1998.

Chambers, Oswald. *My Utmost for His Highest.* New York: Dodd & Mead, 1943.

Cloud, Henry and Townsend, John. *How People Grow.* Grand Rapids: Zondervan Publishing Company, 2001.

Chesterton, G. K. *Orthodoxy.* Garden City, N.Y.: Doubleday/Image Books, 1959.

The Cloud of Unknowing. Author Unknown. Edited by William Johnston. New York: Image Books, 1973.

Coleridge, Samuel Taylor. *Aids to Reflection.* London: William Pickering, 1843.

_______. *The Complete Poetical & Dramatic Works of Samuel Taylor Coleridge.* London: Macmillian and Co., 1893.

Crabb, Larry. *Inside Out*. Colorado Springs: NavPress, 1988.
_______. *The Pressure's Off*. Colorado Springs: WaterBrook Press, 2002.
_______. *Shattered Dreams: God's Unexpected Pathway to Joy*. Colorado Springs: WaterBrook Press, 2001.
Curtis, Brent and Eldredge, John. *The Sacred Romance*. Nashville: Thomas Nelson, 1997.
Day, Dorothy. *Meditations.* New York: The Missionary Society of St. Paul the Apostle in the State of New York, 1970.
Deci Edward L., with Richard Flaste. *Why We Do What We Do: Understanding Self-Motivation*. New York: Penguin Books, 1995.
Demarest, Bruce. *Satisfy Your Soul*. Colorado Springs: NavPress, 1999.
_______. *Soul Guide: Following Jesus as a Spiritual Director*. Colorado Springs: NavPress, 2003.
Di Cesare, Mario A. Editor. *George Herbert and the Seventeenth-Century Religious Poets.* New York: W.W. Norton and Company, 1978.
Dillard, Annie. *Holy the Firm*. New York: Harper Colophon Books, 1977.
_______. *Living By Fiction*. New York: Harper Colophon Books, 1982.
Donne, John. *The Complete English Poems.* New York: Penguin Books, 1971.
The Early Christian Fathers. Edited and translated by Henry Bettenson. Oxford: Oxford University Press, 1956.
Eldredge, John. *The Journey of Desire*. Nashville: Thomas Nelson, 2000.
_______. *Waking the Dead: The Glory of a Heart Fully Alive*. Nashville: Thomas Nelson Publishers, 2003.
Fenelon, François. *Christian Perfection*. Minneapolis: Bethany, 1975.
_______. *Meditations on the Heart of God.* Translated by Robert J. Edmonson. Brewster, Mass.: Paraclete Press, 1997.
_______. *Talking With God.* Brewster, Mass.: Paraclete Press, 1997.
Flavel, John. *Keeping the Heart*. Grand Rapids: Sovereign Grace Publishers, 1971.
The Forgotten Trinity. The Report of the BCC Study Commission on Trinitarian Doctrine Today. Volume I. London: British Council of Churches, Inter-Church House, 1989.
Fosdick, Harry Emerson. *Living Under Tension*. London: Student Christian Movement Press, 1941.
_______. *The Meaning of Faith*. New York: Association Press, 1918.
_______. *The Meaning of Prayer*. New York: Association Press, 1916.
_______. *The Meaning of Service*. New York: Association Press, 1921.
_______. *On Being A Real Person*. New York: Harper & Brothers Publishers, 1943.
_______. *Twelve Tests of Character*. New York: Association Press, 1930.
Foster, Richard J. *Celebration of Discipline.* Second Edition. San Francisco: Harper Collins, 1988.

_______. *Freedom of Simplicity.* San Francisco: Harper & Row, Publishers, 1981.

_______. *Money, Sex & Power*. San Francisco: Harper & Row, Publishers, 1985.

_______. *Prayer: Finding the Heart's True Home.* San Francisco: Harper and Row, Publishers, 1978.

_______. *Seeking the Kingdom: Devotions for the Daily Journey of Faith.* San Francisco: Harper SanFrancisco, 1995.

_______. *Streams of Living Water.* San Francisco: Harper San Francisco, 1992.

Foster, Richard J. and Emilie Griffin, Editors. *Spiritual Classics.* San Francisco: Harper San Francisco, 2000.

Foster, Richard J. and Smith, James Bryan, Eds. *Devotional Classics.* San Francisco: Harper San Francisco, 1993.

France, R. T. *Matthew: Tyndale New Testament Commentaries.* Grand Rapids: William B. Eerdmans Publishing Company, 1985.

Francis de Sales. *Introduction to the Devout Life.* New York: Image, 1972.

Gilbert, Roberta M. *Extraordinary Relationships: A New Way of Thinking About Human Interactions.* Minneapolis: Chronimed Publishing, 1992.

Gordon, S. D. *Quiet Talks on Power.* New York: Fleming H. Revell Company, 1903.

Hammarskjöld, Dag. *Markings.* Translated by Leif Sjoberg & W.H. Auden. New York: Alfred A. Knopf, 1964.

Head, David. *He Sent Leanness.* New York: The Macmillan Company, 1959.

_______. *Shout for Joy.* New York: The Macmillan Company, 1962.

Herbert, George. *The Complete English Poems.* New York: Penguin, 1991.

Hopkins, Gerard Manley. *The Major Poems.* London: Everyman's Library, 1979.

_______. *Poems of Gerard Manley Hopkins.* London: Oxford University Press, 1918.

Hurnard, Hannah. *Hind's Feet on High Places.* Wheaton: Tyndale House Publishers, Inc., 1977.

Hunt, Morton. *The Story of Psychology.* New York: Anchor Press, 1994.

Ignatius of Loyola. *The Spiritual Exercises.* Translated by Anthony Mottola. New York: Image, 1964.

Inge, W. R. *Mysticism in Religion.* London: Hutchinson's University Library, [n.d.].

Juliana of Norwich. *The Revelations of Divine Love.* Translated with an introduction by M.L. del Mastro. New York: Image Books, 1977.

Kagawa, Toyohiko. *The Challenge of Redemptive Love.* New York: Abingdon Press, 1940.

_______. *A Grain of Sand.* New York: Abingdon Press, 1936.

_______. *Meditations*. New York: Harper & Row, Publishers, 1950.
Kauz, Herman. *A Path to Liberation: A Spiritual and Philosophical Approach to the Marital Arts*. Woodstock, New York: Overlook Press, 1992.
Kelly, Thomas R. *The Eternal Promise*. New York: Harper & Row, Publishers, 1966.
_______. *A Testament of Devotion*. San Francisco: Harper San Francisco, 1992.
Kierkegaard, Søren. *Christian Discourses, Etc.* Translated by Walter Lowrie. Princeton: Princeton University Press, 1971.
_______. *Fear and Trembling and Sickness Unto Death*. Translated by Walter Lowrie. Princeton: Princeton University Press, 1941.
_______. *For Self-Examination and Judge for Yourselves!* Translated by Walter Lowrie. Princeton: Princeton University Press, 1941.
_______. *The Journals of Søren Kierkegaard:* A Selection Edited and Translated by Alexander Dru. London: Oxford University Press, 1938.
_______. *The Last Years: Journals 1853-1855.* Edited and Translated by Ronald Gregor Smith. New York: Harper & Row, Publishers, 1965.
_______. *Parables of Kierkegaard.* Edited by Thomas C. Oden. Princeton, N.J.: Princeton University Press, 1978.
_______. *The Prayers of Søren Kierkegaard.* Edited by Perry D. LeFevre. Chicago: University of Chicago Press, 1956.
_______. *Purity of Heart Is To Will One Thing.* Translated by Douglas V. Steere. New York: Harper and Brothers Publishers, 1938.
_______. *Training in Christianity*. Translated by Walter Lowrie. Princeton: Princeton University Press, 1947.
_______. *Works of Love.* Translated by Howard and Edna Hong. New York, Harper & Row, Publishers, 1962.
King, Jr., Martin Luther. *Strength To Love*. Glasgow: Fount, 1963.
_______. *Stride Toward Freedom*. New York: Harper & Row Publishers, 1958.
Kinnard, G. Steve. *The Beginning of Wisdom*. New York: The New York City Church of Christ, 1988.
_______. *The Call of the Wise: An Introduction and Topical Index to the Book of Proverbs.* Waltham, Massachusetts: Discipleship Publications International, 1997.
_______. *The Crowning of the King: A Practical Exposition of the Gospel of Matthew.* Newton, Massachusetts: Illuminations Publishers International, 2004.
_______. *The Final Act: A Biblical Look at End-Time Prophecy.* Waltham, Massachusetts: Discipleship Publications International, 2000.
_______. *Getting the Most From the Bible.* Waltham, Massachusetts: Discipleship Publications International, 2000.

_______. *The Gospel of Mark: An Introduction to Discipleship*. Waltham, Massachusetts: Discipleship Publications International, 1995.

_______. *Holy Land Tour: The Gihon Spring.* (Video). New City, New York: G. Steve Kinnard, 2000.

_______. *Jerusalem: City of Promise.* (Video). New City, New York: G. Steve Kinnard, 1999.

_______. *New Wineskins: Formation of a Ministry of Multimedia Education Integrating the Bible, Geography and Archaeology*. New City, New York: G. Steve Kinnard, 1999.

_______. *Prophets: The Voices of Yahweh.* Waltham, Massachusetts: Discipleship Publications International, 2001.

LaCugna, Catherine Mowry. *God With Us*. San Francisco: Harper San Francisco, 1991.

Lamont, Anne. *Traveling Mercies: Some Thoughts on Faith.* New York: Pantheon Books, 1999.

Lane, George A. *Christian Spirituality—An Historical Sketch.* Chicago: Loyola Press, 1984.

Laubach, Frank C. *Prayer: The Mightiest Force in the World.* New York: Fleming H. Revell Company, [n.d.].

Law, William. *A Serious Call to a Devout and Holy Life.* Grand Rapids: William B. Eerdmans Publishing Company, 1966.

Leupp, Roderick T. *Knowing the Name of God: A Trinitarian Tapestry of Grace, Faith and Community*. Downers Grove: InterVarsity Press, 1996.

Lewis, C. S. *Christian Reflections*. Grand Rapids: William B. Eerdmans Publishing Company, 1967.

_______. *The Chronicles of Narnia: The Lion, The Witch and the Wardrobe.* New York: Harper Collins Publishing, 1950.

_______. *God in the Dock: Essays on Theology and Ethics.* Grand Rapids: William B. Eerdmans Publishing Company, 1972.

_______. *A Grief Observed.* New York: Seabird, 1961.

_______. *The Great Divorce.* New York: Macmillan Publishing Co., Inc., 1946.

_______. *Mere Christianity.* New York: Macmillan, 1956.

_______. *Miracles: A Preliminary Study*. London: Geoffrey Bles, Ltd., 1947.

_______. *The Pilgrim's Regress*. Grand Rapids, Mich., William B. Eerdmans Publishing Co., 1933.

_______. *Poems.* London: Geoffrey Bles, Ltd., 1964.

_______. *The Problem of Pain*. New York: Macmillan, 1962.

_______. *The Screwtape Letters.* New York: Macmillan, 1943.

_______. *Surprised by Joy: The Shape of My Early Life*. New York: Harcourt, Brace and World, 1955.

_______. *The Weight of Glory and Other Addresses.* Grand Rapids: Eerdmans, 1965.

_______. *The World's Last Night and Other Essays.* New York: Harcourt Brace & Company, 1960.

MacDonald, Gordon. *Ordering Your Private World.* Nashville: Oliver Nelson, 1984.

Maliszewshi, Michael. *Spiritual Dimensions of the Martial Arts.* Rutland, Vermont: Charles E. Tuttle Company, 1996.

Manning, Brennan. *A Ragamuffin Gospel.* Sisters, Oregon: Multnomah Publishers Inc., 1990.

_______. *Ruthless Trust.* San Francisco: Harper SanFrancisco, 2000.

May, Gerald G. *Addiction and Grace.* San Francisco: Harper SanFrancisco, 1988.

_______. *The Dark Night of the Soul.* San Francisco: Harper SanFrancisco, 2004.

_______. *Will and Spirit: A Contemplative Psychology.* San Francisco: Harper SanFrancisco, 1982.

Maxwell, John C. *Be A People Person.* Colorado Springs: Victor Books, 1994.

McGrath, Alister. *Spirituality in an Age of Change.* Grand Rapids: Zondervan, 1994.

_______. *The Unknown God: Searching For Spiritual Fulfillment.* Grand Rapids: William B. Eerdmans Publishing Company, 1999.

McNeil, Donald P., Douglas A. Morrison and Henri J.M. Nouwen. *Compassion: A Refection of the Christian Life.* Garden City, New York: Doubleday & Company, Inc., 1982.

Meister Eckhart. *Meister Eckhart: A Modern Translation.* New York: Harper & Row, 1941.

Merton, Thomas. *Contemplative Prayer.* New York: Image, 1969.

_______. *New Seeds of Contemplation.* New York: New Directions, 1961.

_______. *The Seven Storey Mountain.* New York: Harcourt, Brace, and Company, Inc., 1948.

_______. *Spiritual Direction and Contemplation.* Collegeville, Minnesota: Liturgical Press, 1960.

Miller, Calvin. *The Finale.* Downers Grove: InterVarsity Press, 1979.

_______. *The Singer.* Downers Grove: InterVarsity Press, 1977.

_______. *The Song.* Downers Grove: InterVarsity Press, 1975.

Miller, Donald. *Blue Like Jazz.* Nashville: Thomas Nelson Publishers, 2003.

Miller, Keith. *Habitation of Dragons.* Waco, Texas: Word Books, Publishers, 1970.

Moose, Candace C. *The Grateful Heart: Diary of A Heart Transplant.* Cold Spring Harbor, New York: Rosalie Ink Publications, 2005.

Mother Teresa of Calcutta. *A Gift For God: Prayers and Meditations.* San Francisco: Harper & Row, Publishers, 1975.

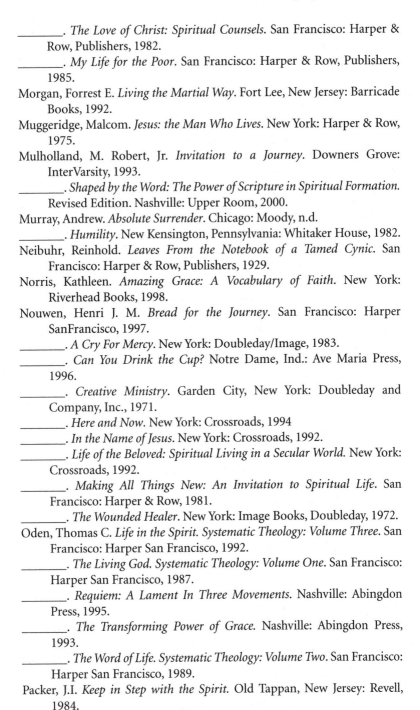

_______. *The Love of Christ: Spiritual Counsels.* San Francisco: Harper & Row, Publishers, 1982.

_______. *My Life for the Poor.* San Francisco: Harper & Row, Publishers, 1985.

Morgan, Forrest E. *Living the Martial Way.* Fort Lee, New Jersey: Barricade Books, 1992.

Muggeridge, Malcom. *Jesus: the Man Who Lives.* New York: Harper & Row, 1975.

Mulholland, M. Robert, Jr. *Invitation to a Journey.* Downers Grove: InterVarsity, 1993.

_______. *Shaped by the Word: The Power of Scripture in Spiritual Formation.* Revised Edition. Nashville: Upper Room, 2000.

Murray, Andrew. *Absolute Surrender.* Chicago: Moody, n.d.

_______. *Humility.* New Kensington, Pennsylvania: Whitaker House, 1982.

Neibuhr, Reinhold. *Leaves From the Notebook of a Tamed Cynic.* San Francisco: Harper & Row, Publishers, 1929.

Norris, Kathleen. *Amazing Grace: A Vocabulary of Faith.* New York: Riverhead Books, 1998.

Nouwen, Henri J. M. *Bread for the Journey.* San Francisco: Harper SanFrancisco, 1997.

_______. *A Cry For Mercy.* New York: Doubleday/Image, 1983.

_______. *Can You Drink the Cup?* Notre Dame, Ind.: Ave Maria Press, 1996.

_______. *Creative Ministry.* Garden City, New York: Doubleday and Company, Inc., 1971.

_______. *Here and Now.* New York: Crossroads, 1994

_______. *In the Name of Jesus.* New York: Crossroads, 1992.

_______. *Life of the Beloved: Spiritual Living in a Secular World.* New York: Crossroads, 1992.

_______. *Making All Things New: An Invitation to Spiritual Life.* San Francisco: Harper & Row, 1981.

_______. *The Wounded Healer.* New York: Image Books, Doubleday, 1972.

Oden, Thomas C. *Life in the Spirit. Systematic Theology: Volume Three.* San Francisco: Harper San Francisco, 1992.

_______. *The Living God. Systematic Theology: Volume One.* San Francisco: Harper San Francisco, 1987.

_______. *Requiem: A Lament In Three Movements.* Nashville: Abingdon Press, 1995.

_______. *The Transforming Power of Grace.* Nashville: Abingdon Press, 1993.

_______. *The Word of Life. Systematic Theology: Volume Two.* San Francisco: Harper San Francisco, 1989.

Packer, J.I. *Keep in Step with the Spirit.* Old Tappan, New Jersey: Revell, 1984.

_______. *Knowing God*. Downers Grove: InterVarsity, 1973.

The Passion of the Christ. Directed by Mel Gibson. Produced by Mel Gibson, Bruce Davey, Stephen McEveety. Icon Productions, 2004.

Payne, Peter. *Martial Arts: The Spiritual Dimension*. New York: Crossroads, 1981.

The Penguin Book of English Christian Verse. Edited by Peter Levi. London: Penguin Books, 1984.

Peters, Ted. *God as Trinity*. Louisville, Kentucky: Westminster/John Knox Press, 1993.

Peterson, Eugene, H. *The Message*. Colorado Springs: NavPress, 2002.

Phillips, J.B. *Your God Is Too Small*. New York: Macmillan, 1961.

The Pixies. "Where Is My Mind?" *Death to the Pixies*. Written by Black Frances. Published by Rice and Beans Music. 4 A.D. 1988.

Pirsiq, Robert M. *Zen and the Art of Motorcycle Maintenance: An Inquiry Into Values*. Los Angeles: Audio Renaissance, 1974.

The Poets' Book of Psalms. Edited by Laurence Wielder. San Francisco: Harper San Francisco, 1995.

Powell, John. *Full Human Fully Alive: A New Life Through a New Vision*. Niles, Illinois: Argus Communications, 1976.

_______. *He Touched Me: My Pilgrimage of Prayer*. Niles, Illinois: Argus Communications, 1974.

_______. *The Secret of Staying in Love*. Niles, Illinois: Argus Communications, 1974.

_______. *Unconditional Love*. Niles, Illinois: Argus Communications, 1978.

Quoist, Michael. *The Breath of Love*. Translated by N.D. Smith. New York: Crossroads, 1987.

_______. *I've Met Jesus Christ*. Translated by J. F. Bernard. Garden City, New York: Doubleday & Company, 1973.

_______. *Prayers*. Translated by Agnes M. Forsyth and Anne Marie de Commaille. New York: Sheed and Ward, 1963.

_______. *With Open Heart*. Translated by Colette Copeland. New York: Crossroads, 1983.

Rahner, Karl. *The Trinity*. Translated by Joseph Doncell. New York: The Crossroad Publishing Co., 1997.

Raines, Robert A. *A Faithing Oak: Meditations From the Mountain*. New York: Crossroads, 1982.

Raposa, Michael L. *Mediation and the Martial Arts*. Charlottesville, Virginia: University of Virginia Press, 2003.

Rauschenbush, Walter. *Christianity and the Social Crisis*. New York: Macmillian Company, 1912.

_______. *For God and the People: Prayers of the Social Awakening*. Boston: The Pilgrim Press, 1909.

_______. *A Gospel for the Social Awakening*. New York: Knickerbocker Press, 1950.

_______. *The Social Principles of Jesus*. New York: Association Press, 1919.

Richardson, Alan D., Editor. *A Theological Word Book of the Bible*. London: SCM Press, Ltd., 1957.

Rienecker, Fritz. Translated by Cleon L. Rogers, Jr. *A Linguistic Key to the Greek New Testament*. Grand Rapids: Zondervan Publishing House, 1976.

Sanders, J. Oswald. *Spiritual Leadership*. Chicago: Moody, 1967.

Scazzero, Peter. With Warren Bird. *The Emotionally Healthy Church*. Grand Rapids: Zondervan Publishing House, 2003.

Schaeffer, Francis A. *The Church At the End of the 20th Century*. Downers Grove: InterVarsity Press, 1970.

_______. *The Church Before the Watching World*. Downers Grove: InterVarsity Press, 1971.

_______. *Escape From Reason*. Downers Grove: InterVarsity Press, 1968.

_______. *The God Who Is There*. Downers Grove: InterVarsity, 1968.

_______. *He Is There and He Is not Silent*. Wheaton: Tyndale, 1972.

_______. *How Should We Then Live? The Rise and Decline of Western Thought and Culture*. Old Tappan, New Jersey: Fleming H. Revell Company, 1976.

_______. *The Mark of A Christian*. Downers Grove: InterVarsity Press, 1976.

_______. *True Spirituality*. Wheaton: Tyndale, 1972.

Shaw, Scott. *The Warrior Is Silent*. Rochester, Vermont: Inner Traditions, 1998.

Smedes, Lewis B. *Forgive and Forget: Healing the Hurts We Don't Deserve*. San Francisco: Harper San Francisco, 1984.

Smith, F. LaGard. *Meeting God in Quiet Places: The Cotswold Parables*. Eugene, Oregon: Harvest House Publishers, 1992.

Smith, Hannah Whitall. *The Christian's Secret Of A Happy Life*. Gainesville, Florida: Bridge-Logos Publishers, 1998.

Sorg, Theo. "Heart," in *The New International Dictionary of New Testament Theology*. Vol. II, Edited by Colin Brown. Grand Rapids: Zondervan Publishing House, 1976.

St. John of the Cross. *Dark Night of the Soul*. New York: Image, 1959.

St. Teresa of Avila. *A Life of Prayer*. Abridged and Edited by James M. Houston. Portland: Multnomah Press, 1983.

Stott, John R. W. *Christian Counter-Culture: The Message of the Sermon on the Mount*. Downers Grove: InterVarsity, 1978.

Suino, Nicklaus. *Arts of Strength, Arts of Serenity: Martial Arts Training for Mental, Physical, and Spiritual Health*. New York: Weatherhill, 1996.

Teresa of Avila. *The Interior Castle*. The Classics of Western Spirituality. New York: Paulist Press, 1979.

A Testament of Hope: The Essential Writing of Martin Luther King, Jr. Edited by James M. Washington. San Francisco: Harper & Row, Publishers, 1986.

Theological Dictionary of the New Testament. Gehard Kittel and Gerhard Friedrick, Editor. Geoffrey W. Bromiley, Translator. Grand Rapids: Wm. B. Eerdmans Publishing Co., 1968.

A Theological Wordbook of the Bible. Alan Richardson, Editor. New York: Macmillan Publ., Co., Inc., 1976.

Thomas a Kempis. *The Imitation of Christ.* Translated by William C. Creasy. Notre Dame, Indiana: Ave Maria Press, 1989.

Thompson, Francis. *The Hound of Heaven and Other Poems.* Boston: International Pocket Library, 2000.

Thompson, John. *Modern Trinitarian Perspectives.* Oxford: Oxford University Press, 1994.

Thoreau, Henry David. *Walden; or, Life in the Woods and On the Duty of Civil Disobedience.* New York: Rinehart & Col, Inc., 1960.

Thurston, Bonnie. *Spiritual Life in the Early Church: The Witness of Acts and Ephesians.* Minneapolis: Fortress Press, 1993.

Tolkien, J.R.R. *The Lord of the Rings.* Second Edition. Boston: Houghton Mifflin Company Boston, 1965.

Tolstoy, Leo. *My Confession, My Religion, The Gospel in Brief.* New York: Thomas Y. Crowell, Co., 1899.

Tozer. A.W. *Man the Dwelling Place of God.* Harrisburg, Pennsylvania: Christian Publications, 1959.

_______. *The Knowledge of the Holy.* New York: Harper and Row, 1961.

_______. *The Pursuit of God.* Harrisburg, Pennsylvania: Christian Publications, 1948.

Underhill, Evelyn. *The Essentials of Mysticism and Other Essays* Oxford: Oneworld Publications, 1999.

_______. *Life as Prayer.* Harrisburg, Pennsylvania: Morehouse Press, 1946.

_______. *Mysticism.* New York: Image, 1990.

_______. *Worship.* New York: Harper & Brothers, 1936.

Wangerin, Jr., Walter. *The Book of the Dun Cow.* San Francisco: Harper & Row, Publishers, 1978.

_______. *The Book of Sorrows.* San Francisco: Harper & Row, Publishers, 1985.

_______. *The Manger is Empty: Stories in Time.* San Francisco: Harper & Row, Publishers, 1989.

_______. *A Miniature Cathedral.* San Francisco: Harper & Row, Publishers, 1987.

_______. *Miz Lil & The Chronicles of Grace.* San Francisco: Harper & Row, Publishers, 1988.

_______. *Paul: A Novel.* San Francisco: Harper & Row, Publishers, 2000.

Wardle, Terry. *The Transforming Path: A Christ-Centered Approach to Spiritual Formation.* Siloam Springs, Arkansas: Leafwood Publishers, 2003.

Warren, Rick. *The Purpose Driven Life.* Grand Rapids: Zondervan Publishing House, 2002.

Weil, Simone. *Waiting for God.* Translated by Emma Craufurd. New York: Harper Colophon Books, 1973.

Westerhoff, John H. *Spiritual Life: The Foundation for Preaching and Teaching.* Louisville, Kentucky: Westminster John Knox Press, 1994.

Willard, Dallas. *The Divine Conspiracy.* San Francisco: Harper San Francisco: 1998.

_______. *Hearing God: Developing A Conversational Relationship With God.* Downers Grove: InterVarsity, 1984.

_______. *Renovation of the Heart.* San Francisco: Harper and Row, 1988.

_______. *The Spirit of the Disciplines.* San Francisco: Harper & Row, 1988.

"*The With-God Life: The Dynamics of Scripture for Christian Spiritual Trans^Formation: A RENOVARE International Conference on Spiritual Renewal,*" *Conference Notebook.* Englewood, Colorado: Renovare, 2005.

Woolman, John. *The Journal of John Woolman.* Boston: Houghton Mifflin Company, 1871.

Wright, N.T. *Colossians and Philemon,* Tyndale New Testament Commentaries. Grand Rapids: William B. Eerdmans Publishing Company, 1986.

Yancey, Philip. *Church: Why Bother.* Grand Rapids: Zondervan Publishing House, 1998.

_______. *Disappointment With God.* Grand Rapids: Zondervan Publishing House, 1988.

_______. *Finding God In Unexpected Places.* Nashville: Moorings, 1995.

_______. *The Jesus I Never Knew.* Grand Rapids: Zondervan Publishing House, 1995.

_______. *Rumors of Another World.* Grand Rapids: Zondervan Publishing House, 2003.

_______. *Soul Survivor: How My Faith Survived the Church.* New York: Doubleday, 2001.

_______. *What's So Amazing About Grace?* Grand Rapids: Zondervan Publishing House, 1997.

Zizioulas, John D. *Being as Communion.* Chrestwood, New Jersey: St. Vladimir's Seminary Press, 1993.

About Illumination Publishers International

Toney Mulhollan has been in Christian publishing for over 30 years. He has served as the Production Manager for Crossroads Publications, Discipleship Magazine/UpsideDown Magazine, Discipleship Publications International (DPI) and on the production teams of Campus Journal, Biblical Discipleship Quarterly, Bible Illustrator and others. He has served as production manager for several printing companies. Toney serves as the Managing Editor of Illumination Publishers International, and is the writer and publisher of the weekly "Behind the Music" stories and edits other weekly newsletters. Toney is happily married to the love of his life, Denise Leonard Mulhollan, M.D.

For the best in Christian writing and audio instruction, go to the Illumination Publishers website. Shipping is always free in the United States. We're commited to producing in-depth teaching that will inform, inspire and encourage Christians to a deeper and more committed walk with God.

www.ipibooks.com

www.ipibooks.com

ipi